ENGLISH AT THE CORE

Open University Press

English, Language, and Education series

General Editor: Anthony Adams
Lecturer in Education, University of Cambridge

TITLES IN THE SERIES

ENGLISH AT THE CORE
Dialogue and power in English teaching

Peter Griffith

Open University Press
Milton Keynes • *Philadelphia*

Open University Press
Celtic Court
22 Ballmoor
Buckingham
MK18 1XW

and
1900 Frost Road, Suite 101
Bristol, PA 19007, USA

First Published 1992

British Library Cataloguing-in-Publication Data

Griffith, Peter
   English at the core: Dialogue and power in
   English teaching. – (English, language, and
   education series)
   I. Title   II. Series
   420.7

   ISBN 0-335-09608-5

Library of Congress Cataloging-in-Publication Data

Griffith, Peter.
   English at the core : dialog and power in English teaching / Peter
Griffith.
     p. cm.
   Includes bibliographical references and index.
   ISBN 0-335-09608-5
   1. English language—Study and teaching (Secondary)—Great
Britain.   I. Title.
LB1631.G767   1991
428′.0071′2041—dc20
                                     91-21241
                                     CIP

Typeset by Graphicraft Typesetters Limited, Hong Kong
Printed in Great Britain by Biddles Limited, Guildford and Kings Lynn

For Diana

Contents

General editor's introduction

Those of us who work in university departments of education sometimes regret the virtual demise of that once staple diet of the PGCE course, some study of the history of education. Though it was never a very popular course with students who failed to see its 'relevance' to their development as young teachers, it is difficult to appreciate where we are in educational practice without some attention also to how we got to where we are now. Peter Griffith's new book provides a fascinating perspective on recent developments in the theory and practice of English teaching, showing, in part, 'some of the ways in which yesterday's hidden curriculum has the disconcerting knack of turning into today's overt political agenda.'

The teaching of English, more than that of any other subject on the school curriculum, is necessarily a political activity. The intention of most English teachers to encourage skills of oral and written expression in their students, to give them power over their own language, is also a teaching that empowers those same students. There have always been those in society who have had an interest in restricting that teaching to minimal competency skills, to enable the young worker to take his or her place in the workplace but to have little ambition beyond this.

Much of the debate over the National Curriculum in English has revolved around two major issues. One of these is the question of the range of literature that should be taught in schools – to what extent the 'canon' needs to be revised to include more contemporary literature drawn from many different cultures. To a large extent the literature read in schools plays a major part in defining a nation's culture; an extension of the canon implies also a redrawing of what we mean by our 'Englishness'. This was most clearly articulated by F. R. Leavis, whose 'Great Tradition' was essentially an articulation of a particular mode of 'Englishness', born out of a continuing puritan ethical tradition.

The other major issue, that of 'Standard English', is equally contentious. To educate students so that they can make a choice as to which form of English they use under particular circumstances should also be to educate them in the way in which the possession and use of the standard English dialect conveys power, and an understanding of the social class-based reasons for this. One virtue of learning more 'knowledge about language' should be to expose the way in which language models society; and to show that issues concerned with race, gender, class, power and control can never be far from the English classroom.

The present volume explores some of these issues. It considers them from a theoretical perspective and also from that of the pedagogy of the classroom. In so doing it reopens some of the debate that was begun many years ago by the publication of Michael Young's *Knowledge and Control*. One of the most significant contributions to that volume was the well-known essay by Basil Bernstein on the classification and framing of educational ideas. The definition of what is meant by knowledge, and the nature of knowledge transmission in the classroom, is a fundamentally important question for educationists, never more so than at a time when, in England and Wales, we are seeing the introduction of a National Curriculum. But such questions are not restricted to the British Isles alone. We have seen in recent years similar attempts in other English-speaking countries to attempt a definition of the legitimate limits of what should be seen as education in one's own language and literature. A recent United States President is reputed to have asked his advisers to try to draw up a list of books that American school students should read in order to encourage them to construct their identity as Americans. The same debates over minimal competency testing are currently taking place in Australia and New Zealand as well as in England and Wales.

To understand the implications of these debates we need the perspectives provided by a number of different academic disciplines. Peter Griffith's contribution to educational thinking in this area draws upon a number of such disciplines, but also makes its own unique contribution. In providing a scaffolding to enable us to understand how we have got to where we are today, it should also lead us to plan more effectively for how we seek to determine the future.

Anthony Adams

Acknowledgements

An early version of Chapter 2 appeared in *English Education*, volume 20, number 4, December 1988, and I am grateful to the editors for their permission to revise and republish it here, and to Gordon M. Pradl and his colleagues for their judicious comments on the original version.

The tapes and transcripts on which much of Chapter 3 is based were used in a presentation to the International Convention on Reading and Response organized by the University of East Anglia in 1989, and I should like to thank the participants in the session for several valuable suggestions, the majority of which I hope I have acted upon. To this must be added my gratitude to colleagues at the Open University for commenting upon an early version of the chapter, and to John Coombes for a spirited commentary upon the whole text.

The writing of this book has been made immeasurably easier by the encouragement and forbearance of my wife and daughters.

The cover illustration is derived from a contemporary representation of a prisoner in a cell in Bentham's proposal for a Panopticon. This present version, as well as substituting a school pupil, also incorporates details drawn from prisons built in the USA on Benthamite principles. These changes reflect the contention of Michel Foucault, discussed in some detail in this book, that the Panopticon provides an analogy to the process of education as it is conducted today.

1 Introduction

This book is about various aspects of the teaching of English, as a school subject, in England and Wales, during the 1990s. As such it cannot afford to be solely about English teaching. It is true that it does a lot of the things that might be expected of a book about the teaching of one particular subject: it deals with the conceptions that people have of what it is about, and what it is for; it looks at some of the teaching styles that have been adopted during the last few decades, and the way in which people have described and envisaged them; it even examines one particular lesson in some detail. But it also recognizes that ideas about total subject autonomy, and the independence of the teacher within the classroom, were never completely consistent with reality, and are now not even plausible. In addition, therefore, to examining English teachers' own conceptions of what they are doing, it tries to relate the present position of the subject to the jumble of motives that underlay the succession of Education Acts and other administrative measures in the United Kingdom during the second half of the 1980s, and to the continuing consequences of these actions, intended and unintended, during the 1990s.

In this pattern of action and reaction, English has certain things in common with other school subjects labelled arts or humanities or aesthetics – the lack of an agreed terminology is perhaps symptomatic of a deeper unpreparedness – but it has the doubtful distinction of being more visible and exposed than most, as a part of the core curriculum on the one hand, and as a haven, it is alleged, of a spurious professionalism and a dangerous progressivism on the other. The temptation therefore exists to represent it as a redoubt which must be defended against the barbarians, and this rhetoric has been deployed at one time or another (though within that span the barbarians have been seen as appearing in various different guises and from various quarters of the compass) throughout most of the relatively short history of the subject. For, like most aspects of our national heritage, it has not been around long, has changed a good deal during that time, and was originally introduced for reasons that would make many of its current practitioners quite properly have second thoughts. These practitioners, moreover, have always included a high proportion of people with no formal qualifications to teach this particular subject – there are some disadvantages, after all, to having a common heritage – and to a considerable degree we lack a general, explicit, and precise agreement as to the reasons why the subject is included in the curriculum, and the benefits it confers on those who study it.

This lack of agreement is well illustrated in the contorted history of the intro-duction of the National Curriculum in England and Wales. The initially privi-leged position of English as a subject was inscribed in the distinction between core and foundation subjects. Many of the opening skirmishes about the nature, scope, validity and utility of testing related to questions of reading and writing. The whittling down of the scope of the National Curriculum for pupils over the age of 14 was one of the first major decisions announced (in early 1991) by Kenneth Clarke as Secretary of State for Education during John Major's premiership. Yet, though its effect was to establish still more firmly the centrality of English within the common curriculum, this major revision was not accompanied by any rationale concerning the subject itself; rather, its position was in some way taken for granted, and such exposition as there was related to the newly increased 'flexibility' in respect of the teaching of subjects such as history and geography.

To the naïve observer, such a privileged centrality might seem to constitute a highly enviable state of affairs. However, it is probably more than ingratitude that causes many English teachers to think that such is not the case. They are aware that the composition of the subject matter that they are responsible for is the subject of fairly intense, though often undeclared, contestation, and that the outcome of their activities is similarly in want of anything approaching a consensual evaluation.

Two of the tasks, therefore, that this book sets itself are to identify and classify some of the notions currently or recently in play as to what English teaching is all about, and to relate these to a particularly overt phase of the struggle for political control of the process of schooling in the United Kingdom. In dealing with the latter point it is of course necessary, as I have already suggested, to step back several paces from one particular school subject, and to examine aspects of educational politics and policies more generally. But these in turn can only be understood within a wider historical and political context, which is occasionally touched on but not exhaustively analysed in this book. Consider, for instance, the brief period of the early to middle seventies. This saw the first oil crisis, the publication of Black Papers, the 1972 and 1974 miners' strikes, and the beginnings of the self-styled 'Great Debate' on education initiated by Callaghan's Ruskin College speech. It would clearly be facile to look to identify one simple common cause for all of these events. Equally, it would be evasive to suggest that fundamental issues of economic growth and prosperity have no connection with workforce planning and the contested identification of economically desirable skills and attitudes, or that the challenge to government posed by organized labour had no bearing on calls for the privatization of educational institutions and the atomization of educational experience.

Part of what this book tries to do, then, is to point towards some connections of this kind, and to trace some of the ways in which yesterday's hidden curriculum has the disconcerting knack of becoming today's overt political agenda. When John Major, introducing an education debate in May 1991, can say, as if uttering a truism, 'I do not want to see young people forced into the system; I want the system to be forced into them', we are forcibly reminded that the nature of discourse about education has changed a great deal in the last two decades or so.

English is a particularly interesting test case here, since its subject matter has been more protean than most, and since it has tended, not only during the 1990s but throughout its fairly brief history, to be perceived by the powers that be as both essential and potentially threatening. It is this ambivalent attitude which probably explains both the large amount of governmental or government-sponsored examination of the subject in the past seventy-five years or so, and the ambiguous or contradictory messages which the results of these examinations have been seen to convey. I will exemplify this point here, though it forms the substance of a later chapter.

The Newbolt Report (Board of Education, 1921) originated in part in a concern that schooling was not producing workers with the necessary basic skills, yet it went a long way towards establishing the notion of the autonomy of English as a freestanding and self-authenticating entity within the curriculum. The Bullock Report (DES, 1975) was commissioned against a background of increasing anxiety about national levels of reading ability, with a particular functional emphasis attached to the possession of this skill, yet it produced a substantial tome that still stands as a waymark on the path to a pupil-centred curriculum. The Kingman Report (DES, 1988a) was widely anticipated to be a corrective to this approach, yet it proved a document that was generally acknowledged as being surprisingly liberal in its tone as well as its conclusions. The National Curriculum Proposals for English (DES, 1988b and 1989) were in turn thought likely to be a reseizing of the ground that Kingman had ceded, but again proved to be (depending on the stance of the observer) either a surprise or a disappointment. All this means that this sequence of documents on English teaching itself provides interesting material for close textual analysis, and Chapter 6 attempts a small amount of work in this potentially very large field.

One possible reaction to this series of publications is that typically adopted by the radical right: yet again the liberal professionals have insinuated their beliefs and their doubts, and have conspired to water down or even sabotage what should have been a root-and-branch reformist measure. This could indeed be one reading of the process of joint investigation and joint authorship of these documents, though the various lists of members of the various committees makes this version of a conspiracy theory a somewhat improbable one. My own interpretation is based on a different assumption. It seems to me that, whilst the position of individuals or of beliefs on a political spectrum can be identified with some accuracy and internal consistency, there is a surprisingly weak correlation between these and what I have called the different subject ideologies of English teaching. Furthermore, there can often be a tenuous connection between a teacher's conscious beliefs and the actual effects that his or her teaching engenders. Thus in Chapter 2, I argue at some length that the 'liberal' approach to English so consistently promotes a form of quiescence and conformism that it can become the functional equivalent of a more overtly conservative approach. Similarly, I suggest at various points that modern versions of conservatism, incorporating both neo-liberal and neo-conservative perspectives, have deeply contradictory attitudes and aims when it comes to considering the place for tradition and the need for skills within the English syllabus, and that this leads them into highly contradictory attitudes towards the subject ideologies of cultural heritage and of the acquisition of skills.

To try to theorize some of these issues, I draw at various times upon the work of two scholars, Bakhtin and Foucault, who have both proved strongly influential in a number of different disciplines. It is, however, difficult to categorize their basic discipline: was Bakhtin a rogue writer on linguistics, or a wildly eccentric sociologist? Was his interest in literature cause or effect of his other explorations? Was Foucault a historian (offstage shouts of 'never!' and 'abominable research work' from many historians), or a philosopher (equal cries of 'unsound' from another direction) – or something else again? 'Unsoundness' is perhaps the quality the two have most in common; it is possible to imagine each of them at various points envying Kierkegaard his coining of the phrase 'Concluding Unscientific Postscript' as the title of a work. And yet each of them was at various times a great believer in system, and engaged on the building of elaborate structures which somehow completely lacked the capacity to be completed. What they did produce, however, were bodies of work that seem likely to remain endlessly stimulating and provocative. By bringing eclectically-chosen methods and observations into improbable juxtaposition, and by deploying a kind of creative fury upon selected Aunt Sallies (psychology for Bakhtin, and a belief in a kind of ameliorative historical progress in the case of Foucault) each was able to map out, often by example rather than by precept, the kind of approach that they found preferable.

Since neither wrote to any great extent on education, it is the easiest rhetorical trick in the world to show that this was really their hidden theme. (Keith Hoskin demonstrates this trick perfectly effectively for one of them in his interesting contribution to Stephen J. Ball's *Foucault and Education* (1990), albeit with his tongue hovering somewhere in the vicinity of his cheek from time to time.) My objective, however, is a more modest one: to use some of Bakhtin's comments on dialogue, and some of Foucault's on the exercise of power, to illuminate some of what goes on when teachers and pupils talk to each other in English lessons. This book, then, is in no way a systematic or comprehensive introduction to the work of either of these two writers. It will have achieved one of its goals, however, if it prompts readers towards such introductions, and thence to the works themselves.

For a good deal of the time, discussion in this book concentrates on what is defined as literature in schools, and on the perceived place of this subject matter within the classroom subject called English. Perceptions of just what this place is have changed and are changing, as the National Curriculum both integrates literature into the wider subject matter and goes some way towards marginalizing it in such a context. The intention here is not uniquely to privilege one particular part of the subject curriculum, but, rather, to examine that aspect of the practice of English teaching which shows up in sharpest relief many of the most contentious aspects of the relationship between subject ideology and its practical implementation. In particular, since literature is in practice to a large extent studied by talking about the works concerned, classroom talk about literature is something in which this book takes a particular interest.

At various times throughout the chapters that follow, reference is made to the categorizations of teaching style and approach that have been found specifically in English classrooms. The problem with such categorizations, useful though they have been and continue to be, is that they often try at the same time to be both descriptive and normative; that is to say, they attempt to offer an analysis of what is going on, and to provide a battle standard around which the scattered troops can rally. Much more sophisticated descriptive grids are offered by, for instance, studies in classroom ethnography. The attractions of the terminology inherited and used by this book, though, is that it has been used fairly consistently from the 1960s to the National Curriculum reports. The consistency, however, relates to occurrence rather than conceptualization – to the terms rather than to their referents – since it is well known that if a word is any good it is worth fighting for. The use of these terms is itself therefore one small part of the subject matter of the book.

Chapter 4 provides a brief account of a larger battle, relating to the introduction and implementation of various pieces of British government legislation during the 1980s. In writing this part of the book, I was aware of the danger of suggesting that the history of a period is the history of its legislation. In fact, as the rest of the book makes clear, I am much more interested in the various local forms of confusion, compromise, struggle and resistance which occur after the stimulus of such legislation, and which, globally speaking, provided the context of reception for such legislation in the first instance. For this reason, analogies with social history rather than political history are probably more appropriate. Chapter 5, in its examination of the actual and potential motifs and motives of English teaching, is a little bit like such a 'social history'. The legislation is part of my subject matter as well, though, because of its direct and unmediated links to the content and management of the curriculum of a kind that is still relatively unfamiliar to us. The continuing interaction in this area promises to be something of recurrent interest. I make no apology, therefore, for adding prediction, and even a little speculation, at this point – even though I am aware of some of the dangers inherent in such an exercise. In view of the continuing high political profile accorded to education, however, I feel I am taking a very low risk in anticipating that questions of this kind will continue to figure prominently in rehearsals of public policy.

Against such large-scale issues of public policy and cultural theory, concentration on one particular part of the curriculum (English), and then on one of its components (literature), and finally on one particular literature lesson in some detail (as I do in Chapter 3) is capable of being seen as the merest parochialism. Alternatively, it could be seen as a concession to the more ungroundedly empirical approach that I take issue with elsewhere from time to time. I prefer to think, however, that it provides a necessary exemplification and testing of the theoretical material that I have decided to introduce. Not, I hasten to add, that either Bakhtin or Foucault could be accused of resorting to a barren and unrelieved abstraction in what they wrote. On the contrary, their particular illustrations are often as memorable as the general contentions that they are designed to sustain.

As far as these general contentions are concerned, I have not assumed a prior knowledge on the part of the reader of any of the works, nor of any of the arguments, that can be attributed to either of these two theorists. On the other hand, I have deliberately chosen not to offer unbroken chapters of pure exposition either. I am aware that this may prove an irritating strategy, or worse, but I have two separate reasons for adopting it. The first is, if you like, a pedagogical one; I hope that the continual contextualizing of the issues, and the recurrence of key points, will be a helpful device for anyone with no previous familiarity with the issues involved. The other is more like a mimetic one; there does not exist a single, pure, source text written by either of these writers that unambiguously lays out a series of key propositions. On the contrary, both adopted elaborate, if differing, means to make such a reading as difficult as possible. In the case of Bakhtin, it is believed by most scholars that he published several of his works under the names of various of his friends. The 'Bakhtin' that I discuss, then, is a composite figure constructed out of texts bearing several different names, and conceivably has no exact relation to a single biological entity. Since I have no competence to adjudicate in these matters, I have simply followed the prevailing convention, and have therefore treated 'Volosinov' as 'Bakhtin' throughout.

Foucault is a different matter. Having published several volumes in his own name, he began to give an extended series of interviews in which he reviewed and commented upon his previous dominant concerns. Since each review provides a slightly different gloss upon the original text, the overall effect is a bit like a palimpsest, continually re-covered with differing inscriptions of the author's name. Since Foucault was himself the producer of a significant essay discussing the death of the author, the result is not without its ironies.

In my own authorial role, however, I would suggest that this present book falls into the category of those that are best read straight through from beginning to end, even though each chapter picks up a new topic and develops it in a way that I hope is tolerably self-contained. This is the traditional (if not the usual) way of doing things, and, equally traditionally, I have completed my text with some conclusions and some recommendations. However, that is not really the end of it at all. Bakhtin said that a book is an utterance and therefore part of a conversation. This book undoubtedly arose from a multiplicity of conversations with English teachers – past colleagues and past and present students – as well as those teachers who kindly let me into their lessons when I was preparing some of this material. I look forward to seeing what they, and others, will say, and do, next.

2 The discourses of English teaching

In this chapter an attempt is made to define and analyse some of the features of the liberal approach to the teaching of English which has been such a significant feature of classroom practice in England and Wales during the past quarter of a century. My use of the word 'significant' is intended to signal two things: the importance of this form of pedagogy as exemplary for, rather than always typical of, the profession during the period in question, and the fact that it now functions as a rallying point in the face of concerted ideological and political action to standardize and regulate the teaching of English.

It is entirely reasonable, in the face of such action, that many teachers of English should feel not only that their professional autonomy in respect of classroom practice is under threat, but also that their capacity to define their subject matter may diminish or disappear. It is not then surprising that many of them currently respond (as was seen in correspondence in the educational press after the publication of the Kingman Report) by emphasizing the virtues of liberalism, autonomy, and individual development that have been the hallmark of so much good classroom practice in the past two decades or so, and that represent the consensual values of what the New Right would doubtless dismiss as the English-teaching Establishment. What this chapter seeks to do is to ask whether such virtues and such values represent the best basis from which resistance to curricular *dirigisme* can be mounted. It does so by looking at some examples of reported classroom practice, and at the historical development of the curricular strategies within which they were formed. I emphasize this last point particularly, since it is a characteristic of liberalism to fail to recognize either that it is historically located, or that it is itself an ideology rather than something merely neutral or self-evident.

However, the history of English as an independent curricular entity in British schooling is a relatively short one, and definitions of the appropriate subject matter and (inextricably interconnected with this) the appropriate pedagogy have proved notoriously unstable. These definitions have also characteristically been, in the popular sense of the term, extremely rhetorical; another way of putting this point would be to say that they have often been highly normative statements, or assertions of how things ought to be, rather than descriptive ones. More purely descriptive accounts of classroom interactions can, to a limited degree, be traced back to nineteenth-century inspectors' reports, but it is only relatively recently that the recording of classroom discourse has been practised as a regular feature both of research studies and of opinion formation within the profession. However, because their value systems are often so overt, it is frequently quite profitable to compare the earlier, uninhibitedly normative statements with more recent descriptive-seeming ones that seem to have been more discreetly uttered. I say 'seem', because one of the indications of the passing of the years is to revisit documents that were new ten or twenty years ago, and to realize now – concretely rather than just theoretically – how much they are in fact historically-located and ideologically-charged texts. This is not to imply, of course, that more recent publications are either written after the end of history or free from various kinds of ideology – indeed, the contrary is the case. But, to take a symptomatic example, I am struck, in the quotations that follow in this chapter, by the quite unselfconsciously exclusive use of 'he' as the third-person pronoun in publications where (reading current practice backwards into the past) I would have felt confident that this would not have been the case.

Let me summarize briefly. The development of popular education in England and Wales during the nineteenth century had much to do with the demand for greater and more widespread proficiency in the performance of reading and, to a lesser extent, writing. To adopt the classification used by Dixon (1967, though I quote in this chapter from the expanded edition of 1975), this was the era in which the transmission of *skills* was accorded the greatest importance. By the early years of the twentieth century, however, an ideology of cultural nationalism, offered in the guise of a liberal reaction against a mechanistic acquisition of skills, had come to predominate. This entailed, amongst other things, the transmission via schooling of selected works from a range of 'national' literature. The spirit of this is well caught in a passage from the Newbolt Report of 1921:

> ... we state what appears to us to be an incontrovertible primary fact, that for English children no form of knowledge can take precedence of a knowledge of English, no form of literature can take precedence of English literature: and that the two are so inextricably connected as to form the only basis possible for a national education. (Board of Education, 1921:14)

The association of cultural nationalism and a common educational system is of course not a phenomenon unique to one country; research by Renée Balibar and also by Blampain have described something of its emergence in France, for example. It forms the second of Dixon's three paradigms, which he describes as being that of the *cultural heritage*.

It might have seemed that this form of education would have been dysfunctional in terms of certain of the stated aims of the previous generation; after all, time spent on the study of literature, whether within a liberal-nationalist framework or otherwise, is time not spent on the acquisition of reading and writing as decontextualized skills. However, the investigations of the Newbolt Committee led it to the conclusion that this was not in fact the case:

> ... what the leading firms of the country desired most of all in their employees were just those qualities which a liberal education, rightly understood, should develop in young people. Indeed, their chief count against the schools was that present-day education was not liberal enough, and, in particular, that it was conventional and divorced from reality. (p. 129)

In the context of reception of the 1990s, these are curious words, and sentiments, to read. 'Liberal' is not now often used as a term of approval by industrialists. 'Conventional', we should note, implies the obeying of conventions rather than the analysing of them. 'Divorced from reality', we may suspect, is in its own way equally a conventional term and equally in need of analysis. It would appear that what is really being alleged here, by people who had a clear stake in the outcomes of the educational process, is that the so-called mechanical exercises of spelling and punctuation were not as effective a means of generating the skills and attitudes which were required by employers as were the reading and guided study of approved literary works. But since it is self-evident that these skills and attitudes do not transfer in any obvious and mechanical sense to the activities conducted on shop-floors and in offices, I would suggest that what is being discussed, and in fairly obvious fashion, is the transmission of a dominant ideology that has certain specifiable and unequally distributed benefits.

The third of Dixon's paradigms, and the one which he tells us was commended by the influential Dartmouth Seminar on which he was reporting, was that of *personal growth*, in which teachers were convinced of 'the need to re-examine the learning processes and the meaning to the individual of what he is doing in English lessons' (1975:1–2). Whether 'learning processes' are in fact the same thing as 'meaning to the individual', and whether meaning is thus unproblematically accessible to the individual consciousness, are questions on which I want to focus. It is, then, this category of Dixon's on which I shall wish to concentrate during the rest of this chapter, but I should like before that to refer briefly to another threefold classification, this time a synchronic rather than a diachronic one, which I think will be useful in deconstructing Dixon's categories.

I am referring here to the French cultural theorist Michel Foucault, and specifically to the process which he calls 'this kind of political "double-bind", which is the simultaneous individualization and totalization of modern power structures' (Foucault, 1982:216). He applies this to education in the following way:

> Take for example an educational institution: the disposal of its space, the meticulous regulations which govern its internal life, the different activities which are organized there ... all these things constitute a block of capacity-communication-power. The activity which ensures apprenticeship and the acquisition of aptitudes

or types of behaviour is developed there by means of a whole ensemble of regulated communications (lessons, questions and answers, orders, exhortations, coded signs of obedience, differentiation marks of the 'value' of each person and of the levels of knowledge) and by the means of a whole series of power processes (enclosure, surveillance, reward and punishment, the pyramidal hierarchy). (pp. 218–19)

There are three terms in play here in Foucault's definition of the 'block'. The first is capacity, which Foucault describes as a process of craftsman-like apprenticeship, the learning of skills and abilities, or how to achieve, in his terms, a 'transformation of the real'. In a technology lesson, for instance, this would involve skills of design and physical manipulation, appropriate both to the immediate purposes of the lesson and to the post-school environment. The second of his terms is communication, and this consists of questions and answers, structured dialogue, the implicit rules of turn-taking and precedence – in short, very much the subject matter adopted by discourse analysis and by conversation analysis. The third term, power, which involves enclosure, surveillance, reward and punishment, is of course the domain which Foucault made very much his own, in his studies of 'total institutions' such as hospitals, asylums, and prisons.

English lessons, in particular those conducted within the paradigm of personal growth, differ from technology lessons in that the 'capacity', the skill that is being learnt, is in fact at the same time the second of Foucault's categories, the skill of successful communication. Thus, communication is the declared subject matter of the lesson, rather than (or perhaps in addition to being) an unspoken aspect of a hidden curriculum. This means that the contest between power and resistance, which Foucault sees as occurring in particular in large institutions such as schools, is in many ways taking place closer to the surface of observation than it is in other school subjects; the ideological polarity comes nearer to being apparent and manifest.

What must now be done is to establish how far these categories that Foucault devised can be helpful in classifying and analysing what goes on in English lessons. Torbe and Protherough, the editors of an anthology of essays on English teaching published in 1976, contrastingly quote in their introduction two ideal-typical English lessons, the first from the early 1960s, the second from ten years later. I should emphasize that these are not pieces of actual classroom observation, though they are abstracted from many hours of such by the practitioners involved.

> The teacher reads aloud some carefully chosen passage of prose or verse . . . something which few of them know already, but which they may come to enjoy with profit . . . Next a part of the passage is read again in fairly short sections, but in each case a word or phrase is omitted and some other word (usually less apt) is substituted, the change being indicated by a change in the reader's voice . . . The pupils are asked to jot down what they judge (or remember) to be the original word . . . The two main advantages of this type of lesson are (1) a detective interest since there is in a limited sense a 'right' answer (2) the opportunity of discussing words,

phrases, rhythms and imagery and all other such matters in an adequate context. (p. 8)

The passage which is offered in contrast to the above runs as follows:

> (a film is shown) The lights go up, the teacher briefly reminds the pupils that he would like them to talk over their impressions . . . and that perhaps they would like to make further notes . . . talking begins . . . the teacher sits in on one group and listens to the conversation. On the whole he is contented just to listen as the pupils respond personally to the film . . . The discussion has now more or less exhausted itself and the teacher, sensing that little further learning would take place, suggests that the class might once more like to see the film . . . The teacher now asks the pupils to try to write about (their impressions). The choice is, in a sense, infinite. This being so, the teacher feels there must be opportunities to write in whatever form each pupil senses appropriate . . . He therefore gives the pupils a choice of writing a poem, a piece of prose, a dramatization . . . (p. 7)

The editors of this book comment that the teachers 'have different views of the authority relationship between teacher and pupils', and at a purely common-sense level one can see the point that is being made; doubtless most of us would prefer to be pupils in the second class rather than in the first. Perhaps, though, even at this common-sense level it would be useful to say that the variation in authority relationship appears more on the teacher/subject matter dimension than on the teacher/pupil one. After all, in the second example the teacher in each case prescribes the activity to be undertaken; he 'senses' when it is time to move on to the next; he 'asks' for a particular activity to be undertaken: in short, the lesson structure, the whole nature, shape, direction and duration of the discourse, is directly under the control of the teacher. And if someone asserts that that is what teaching is all about I can only agree; discourse that is there for some pedagogical purpose is, almost by definition, something that the teacher has prepared or permitted, even if not participated in. The editors of the book seek to draw a distinction between the moderately closed questions to be found in the first passage and the moderately open ones in the second; this is fair comment, but I am still struck by the resemblance between a half-empty glass and a half-full one.

The pedagogy that is in play here is well described by Dixon:

> Sometimes, when the group is working confidently and constructively, the teacher will pick up the talk as if he was another member of the group, leaving the pupils the initiative and merely nudging them on their way. But if a group stumbles over the complex planning involved or fails to see enough of the possibilities, he may need to take on a different role, trying through discreet questions and comments to develop a framework that will help them on their way. (1975:35)

These 'discreet questions and comments', and the presupposition that there is a 'way' along which the pupils are to be helped, are well enough illustrated in the following teacher-led discusssion in a classroom in the 1970s. The poem under discussion is a translation of 'The Companion' by Yevtushenko. Here, and throughout, I have reproduced the conventions of transcription of the original publication. In this instance *T* is the teacher, who appears convinced that 'revenge' is not a concept that will help these pupils on 'their way'.

T: OK. This is a good point. Sharon?

S: I think the girl's quite bossy, really.

T: You think she's bossy – now (murmur).

P: I don't think she's got much understanding with him.

T: Why not?

P: Well, she doesn't seem to have much sympathy – when the boy gets tired.

T: Now – this is a good point – do the rest of you agree with Sharon that the girl hadn't got much sympathy? (murmur 'no')

N: Well, he wasn't very sympathetic with her really, at the start – he was – tags her along – um – and yanks her about, and sort of said – 'come on quickly we'll get out of here'. I think I'd've been the same, really, if she'd bossed me around at the start – I think I'd have done the same to him, when he got tired.

T: Now. Is it just a matter of revenge you see your – what both of you are saying – What Nicholas is saying and what Sharon is saying is that to a certain extent – after a time – the girl getting her revenge on the boy. Is it as simple as that? Is it really just a matter of getting revenge, or not, Gillian?

(P. Williams in Torbe and Protherough, 1976:51)

Williams cites this passage in order to contrast it with another, quoted below, in which the pupils ran their own discussion in the absence of the teacher, and he makes it quite clear that he regards the latter exercise as more pedagogically valuable. However, it is more than just a quibble to observe that in another sense the teacher was not really absent at all, since the discussion was being taped, as the pupils knew, for future analysis. It is not primarily the presence of the technology that is significant here, since pupils adapt to that readily enough, but rather that the discourse is still being contained within the power relationships established by the school context. In this passage each line appears to indicate a new speaker turn in the conversation.

The girl turned out to be braver . . .
I can get further without getting worn out . . .
mmm.
But before long he realizes she's got more courage.
And got more . . .
They're both very small, obviously – very young . . .
mmm . . .
She was nine. The boy was obviously old – older.
Yes.
No. The thing is . . .
She says 'You small boys'.
Yes but – well – she was probably about nine or ten, but he isn't, you know, (murmur) trying to be a man. She's comparing him, really, with a man because she says 'you small boys, you're always trying to be big, like men'.
About eleven or twelve, at the most, I should imagine.

(p. 52)

I hope it will not now be thought too fanciful if I compare certain features of the above passage with Foucault's description of the operation of the Panopticon. The Panopticon, as envisaged by the utilitarian Jeremy Bentham in the closing years of the eighteenth century, consisted of a scheme for supervision and control that, though originally seen as a model prison, was in principle adaptable to all forms of mass social control in which the organization of space and the distribution of activities through time lay within the control of a central monitoring and controlling power. The subjects were ranged in cells around the periphery, and liable to observation from a central monitoring tower, though they would never know whether at any given time that observation was taking place or not. The subjects therefore have to practise self-monitoring, becoming in effect their own first, best gaolers. Since orthodox behaviour can earn approval, and deviant activity can at any time call down punishment, they internalize and put into practice the norms of the institution. The cells are like 'small theatres in which each actor is alone, perfectly individualised and constantly visible' (Foucault, 1977:200).

Of course in the example we are looking at the pupils work in small groups, but this seems to me no more than a refinement of the principle, and one that Bentham came to endorse: there are enough pupils to encourage and control each other's performance, but not enough (or not in a powerful enough position) to develop a deviant and non-acceptable discourse. Swearing might incur punishment, for instance, and silence would certainly generate disapproval as and when these tapes were sampled.

Another observation of Foucault's, however, might seem more difficult to incorporate into the comparison I have been seeking to draw. Each individual, he claims, 'is the object of information, never a subject in communication' (ibid., p. 200). Being denied the status of a subject strips the individual of both autonomy and value.

The whole essence of the 'personal growth' pedagogy is that the pupils, by means of structured interaction with the world in which they live, should arrive at maturity and self-knowledge. Dixon, after presenting a passage about some newts written in diary form by a ten-year-old boy, says

> the language invites a listener and speaks directly to him . . . In sharing the experience with the imaginary listener, he brings it to life again, realises it for himself . . . It is as if he is listening and scanning what he has just said. At other places he has wanted a different kind of communion with the listener . . . It is an open invitation to join him in feeling that life is good. (1975:5)

In other words, being a 'subject in communication' (in Foucault's sense of the phrase) is fundamental to the way that Dixon perceives the organization of this particular discourse. Yet it is important to be clear here just how many things are being communicated, and what degree of importance attaches to each. It is not as though the teacher has acquired some new knowledge about newts that s/he will then proceed to apply. Rather s/he has received confirmation that, on some securely approved topic, such as the observation of nature, the pupil has demonstrated the ability to produce a discourse that conforms to the liberal, individualizing model of personal development that is fundamental to this pedagogy. This is not to say, of course, that either teacher or pupil would be aware of the process in these terms, or that personal growth is somehow an intrinsically bad thing. Rather it is that some messages carry other messages on their backs; the teacher has learned not only that the pupil's intellectual and affective development proceeds apace, but that her/his curriculum and pedagogy have been collaborated with rather than challenged.

Barnes, dealing in 1971 with some aspects of the question I have just raised, says that:

> In every classroom it is the teacher who finally controls what counts as valid knowledge. In order to succeed, pupils have at least temporarily to take over their teachers' various frames of reference and some are less successful at this than others. A pupil's out-of-school reality may be very different from that of his teacher, who is often quite unaware of this . . . Some teachers, however, are able to draw pupils more actively into the formulating of knowledge, so that what is accepted as valid in that classroom is the result of negotiation between teacher and pupil. If this raises the value of their contribution in the pupils' own eyes it is likely to enable them to join more actively in learning. Every child, given the right topic and the right social relationships, can be helped to use language in the struggle to sort out something for himself or for someone else who really wants to know. (*Times Educational Supplement* cited in Torbe and Protherough, 1976:57–8)

This seems to me the most perceptive aspect of the liberal discourse of English teaching, acknowledging real institutional and social constraints, and realistically planning to overcome some of them. A less acceptable, if more robust, one appears in the following description of the activities of English teachers:

> They have resisted the divisions of labour encoded in the different technical grammars of the culture by attempting to find and speak up for 'a central, a truly human point of view'. They have – under the impulse, no doubt, of *Scrutiny* – located that centrality in the suburban backgarden of liberal individualism. There are worse places for it to be. These teachers have taught the primacy of the individual sensibility, the unflinching need to keep your private self your own and clear, spontaneous, intelligible, and full of life. (F. Inglis in Torbe and Protherough, 1976:173)

What this declaration manifestly does not address is the question of whether the 'need' to preserve the private self is capable of being translated into accomplishment simply by being 'taught' enough; the wish is not always father to the deed. The imagery of the passage is revelatory as well as systematic: we are to eschew the 'division of labour' (with its connotations of the world of work) and 'technical grammars' (which suggest both vocational and related academic forms of specialization) in order to achieve a 'centrality' which is immediately decentred by being located in the suburbs, comfortably distanced from both the factory and the academy. The passage is both defensive about the tradition from which it springs – the Leavisite diatribe against 'mass civilization' in favour of 'minority culture' – and yet triumphalist in its assertion of its definition of humanity. Leavis's own slogan 'We were Cambridge in spite of Cambridge' enacts (if one may apply a technical grammar to the utterance) precisely this process of decentred centrality.

For what I would take to be an example of this approach in practice, 'keeping your private self your own and clear', consider the following transcript. The teacher who recorded himself was on the whole pleased with his strategy as constituting good teaching through the medium of discussion. The poem that the group have just read is Ted Hughes's 'The Jaguar', which contains a vivid description of the eponymous beast pacing its cage. The resemblance of this theme to some of the earlier passages in this chapter dealing with the observation of subjects in cells is happy but fortuitous. *T* is the teacher, and *G* and *B* refer to girl and boy pupils.

> *G1:* At first I thought it wasn't in a zoo and then when Jane put the question, reading it through again I realized that it was in a zoo – 'cage after cage' – and we looked into it further.
>
> *G2:* It dealt with animals in this one and the last one was people. We understand people more than animals because – you know – they got minds.
>
> *T:* Well, some would say it's about animals. Could all this apply to people?
>
> *B1:* This could apply to criminals locked up in jail – the jaguar's like a new cell mate – he's just come from the outside world and wants to get back out again – his thirst for freedom. He's trying to get out, you know. The others have just given up trying – served their sentence.
>
> *T:* Yes, it could refer to people. The idea that – don't give in, don't let the system beat you – that you're still a person, that your imagination and your spirit can take you wherever you want to go. So in some ways it's not just about animals.
>
> (J. Alcock in Torbe and Protherough, 1976:69–70)

I am impressed by the ability of *G2* to sustain the realist and realistic observation that animals are different from people and that it is the latter that we have some chance of understanding; both the teacher and, to some degree, the text are after all trying to drive her to a contrary conclusion. She is, did she but know it, a true adherent of the tradition in social science that runs from the eighteenth-century philosopher Vico, who asserted that we cannot fully understand the world of nature since it is the handiwork of God, whereas we can comprehend society since it is made by man.

But, if she resists the force of the poem and of the lesson by sustaining this realistic interpretation, it is the teacher who first suggests that the poem may deal metaphorically with human experience – 'Could all this apply to people?' – and then represents this as the pupils' discovery – 'Yes, it could refer to people'.

B1 accepts the metaphorical force of the poem when the possibility is put to him – 'This could apply to criminals locked up in jail' – but he represents the animal's/prisoner's response as a wish to escape – 'wants to get back out again' – and a determination to do so – 'He's trying to get out, you know'.

The teacher appears to accept these remarks, but their specificity is lost in his more general reference to the force of the metaphor of animal/human experience. When he returns to the theme – 'don't give in, don't let the system beat you' – he endorses the notion of resistance, but his next move is to valorize the liberal generalization of human essence – 'you're still a person' – whilst confining the notion of resistance to a purely internal and spiritual event which challenges everything and changes nothing – 'your imagination and your spirit can take you wherever you want to go'. This is the process of the simultaneous individualization and totalization of modern power structures to which Foucault was referring; the teacher's strategy inculcates and endorses the notion of the non-conformist isolate, whilst at the same time confirming that society is overwhelmingly stronger. It is reasonable also to suppose that the contemporary equivalents to the employers surveyed by the members of the Newbolt Committee in 1921 would also feel that this mode of education was sufficiently 'wedded to reality' to meet the purposes that they had in mind; that 'reality', after all, read off a dominating and homogeneous society from the structures of the cultural 'common heritage'.

The processes of imaginative response and adaptation to new ideological structures in such circumstances is often given the name of creativity. Torrance (1962) defined the psychological preconditions for such mental processes in the following way:

1 The absence of serious threat to the self, the willingness to risk.
2 Self-awareness – in touch with one's feelings.
3 Self-differentiation – seeing self as being different from others.
4 Both openness to the ideas of others and confidence in one's perceptions of reality or in one's own ideas.
5 Mutuality in interpersonal relations – balance between excessive quest for social relations and pathological rejection of them.

The significant feature of this list is the way in which it both constitutes the individual as a social isolate and renders him/her liable to the influence of the dominant ideology, whilst representing this proceeding as nothing more than the fair exchange of ideas in the intellectual market-place. However, Alcock's treatment of these categories, in the essay quoted above, consists of an assertion that they describe how 'the conscious self is freed from inhibition and external domination' – or, as I should prefer to put it, both perceived internal and perceived external constraints are made to disappear, whilst the individual is the more thoroughly exposed to a reworking of fundamental concepts. Alcock's description of this process reads somewhat differently:

Where the pupils' questions fail, the teacher's must encourage, guide, stimulate. Such questions should open the way to discovery; they should not test or instruct directly, although students learn how to enquire both by inquiring themselves and by observing others do so, and teachers' questions can be a guide to the enquiry process. (p. 63)

What I have been trying to argue is that 'not testing or instructing directly' may, without the teacher's knowledge, be a more effective means of inculcating a repressive ideology than a direct approach would have been. Since most of the points that I have been trying to establish in this chapter, moreover, have consisted of a critique of liberal pedagogy, it is essential to stress that I am not in the business of arguing for some new and different pedagogy of hyper-liberalism in which the teacher will magically rise to new heights of ideological non-interference and purity. Rather I am arguing that it is important for teachers to have an increased awareness of the effects and the effectiveness of the discourse which earns them their daily bread. So long as they believe that their activities are essentially neutral as social practices, they will continue to produce powerful social results all unawares. And, if a new and overtly right-wing curriculum introduces a heavy ideological bias under the guise of raising standards, improving work skills, and re-establishing traditional values, then the arguments in favour of personal development as an all-sufficient pedagogy cannot be sufficiently effective against this new populism.

It is insufficiently effective, I think, because personal growth has frequently (though not invariably) tended to be construed as individual in an atomistic sense – as a developmental process which can be helped or hindered by class-room material and classroom conversation, but in which the social dimension is often weak and occasionally negligible. The 'suburban backgarden' of Inglis's metaphor was a revealing instance of this: in cultivating your garden you probably chat to your immediate neighbours, but you can hardly set up a community council. What English teachers might now profitably attempt to do is to work with a much more dialogic and social model of language, learning, and personal growth, and one which fully recognizes the constraints of the institutional nexus of the school, the curriculum, and the state.

In Foucault's imagery, the only counterpoise to power is resistance, which is a term to which he gave a moderately precise definition to which I shall return later. However, as I have been describing some of the instances of the manifestation of power, it would seem at least mildly cheering to end with an example of resistance taking place. In Alcock's lesson transcription I was particularly taken with the following:

T: Alan, are there any questions which you feel ought to be asked now? Have we made this poem, which you understood as simple and straightforward, too complicated?

B1: No. I understand it as it was when I first read it and I understand it now, as I read it now, with all the questions that have been asked.

(p. 70)

This is offered to us as an example of a frequently non-cooperative, possibly even recalcitrant, pupil, normally unwilling to chance his arm or participate in the give-and-take of classroom debate. Even taken at its face value, however, the response, in its written form at least, is ambiguous: does Alan now accept a multi-layered interpretation, or is he simply bracketing off all discussion subsequent to his original reading? The teacher appears to assume the second possibility to be the case. Where one observer sees a failure according to the standards of the liberal ideal, however, it is possible for an alternative analysis to discover an altogether admirable refusal of a dominant ideology. It seems to me that it is the business of the English teacher to be in there also.

3 Much ado about English

In this chapter I want to look in more detail at one particular English literature lesson. It is one that I myself observed and recorded some fifteen years or so after the majority of the lessons referred to in the previous chapter took place. Like them, I would imagine, it is characterized by a friendly and trusting relationship between teacher and pupils, and by an openness that accommodated itself to my inquiries. Both parties agreed to my being present to tape the lesson, and to three subsequent visits in which I took on a more active role as interviewer. My first session was with the teacher alone, and my second with the original group of pupils, plus one returner from absence, but minus, unfortunately, one active participant in the taped lesson. The last session, following almost immediately on the preceding one, reunited the group with the teacher.

Prior to my session alone with the teacher, she was able to replay the complete recording of the lesson to herself. I had intended that the group of pupils should do the same, but practical difficulties prevented this. For each of the interview sessions, however, I prepared transcripts of short sequences from the original lesson, and distributed them to be read in conjunction with the playing of the relevant taped extracts. At this stage I attempted to be as non-directive as possible, and concentrated on inviting the participants to comment on any features that seemed to be of interest to them. Later in each session I became more directive, often challenging them to comment on quite brief utterances, and permitting myself to ask supplementary questions. The final session was thus inevitably different in kind, both because of an element of recursiveness in the questioning, and because of a quite different set of group dynamics in which the formats of lesson and investigation intersected.

As in my discussion in the previous chapter, I was interested in the differing meanings of words used in dialogue between teacher and pupils, and a further set of differences in meaning between the written literary text and the discussion that ensues from it. And, since I was looking at a variant of the old assertion that knowledge is power – in this case, a reformulation that would run something like 'Power consists of the generation of the dominant set of meanings' – I was also concerned to try to study the interrelationship of micro- and macro-levels of dominance.

I want to draw primarily on two different theoretical perspectives on these themes, and the first of these, that of Foucault, I have already referred to in the previous chapter. The second is derived from a text that has become increasingly familiar to a number of English teachers, amongst other people, in the past decade or so. I am referring here to the volume published under the title *Marxism and the Philosophy of Language*, and under the name of V. N. Volosinov. Since this is now generally recognized to have been written by M. M. Bakhtin, I shall refer to the latter henceforward as the author. I shall also at this stage give no more than a relatively sketchy account of the theoretical area that Bakhtin was laying out, and concentrate on a few of the key terms involved.

For Bakhtin the origin of language was in dialogue – indeed, for him, all language uses are at bottom dialogic – and the analytical unit of speech on which research has to focus is not the word or the sentence, but the utterance. The definition of an utterance is something that Bakhtin works away at continuously; it is a complete unit of speech rather than a component of language, and participants in dialogue work to formulate their own, and to recognize others', utterances. In the end, the definition is very much like the famous one of an elephant – you recognize one when you see one – and Bakhtin quotes a passage in Dostoyevsky's *Diary of a Writer* which describes six workmen in the street, each uttering no more than a common and very basic expletive, but, by dint of differing intonation, and also as a consequence of the placing of each utterance within the sequence of the dialogue, contriving to generate very different meanings (Bakhtin, 1929:103–4).

This virtuoso performance may be considered a co-operative effort, which indeed all dialogue is to some extent, but Bakhtin also draws attention to those instances where meaning is the subject of contest. This contest is not merely random or narrowly interpersonal, since 'every sign is subject to the criteria of ideological evaluation (i.e., whether it is true, false, correct, fair, good, etc.)' (p. 10).

Furthermore, this concatenation of signs is itself the origin of consciousness, which 'takes shape and being in the material of signs created by an organized group in the process of its social intercourse' (p. 13). This 'organized group' is what gives each particular usage of a sign system its distinctive quality: 'the forms of signs are conditioned above all by the social organization of the participants involved and also by the immediate conditions of their interaction' (p. 21). And, since the participants can have different backgrounds and different interests, the sign system can become an arena of struggle. It is this polyvocality of the sign which distinguishes it from a signal, since the latter is characterized by its univocality and lack of context dependence.

I want to apply these comments to the acting-out of the relationship between, and the series of spoken utterances produced by, the teacher and pupils that I outlined above. But it should be noted that Bakhtin's comments deal not only with signs that are currently the site of struggle, but also with those that have retired from the fray, 'degenerating into allegory and becoming the object not of live social intelligibility but of philological comprehension' (p. 23). To the extent that words in some literary texts – texts that do not 'speak' to a present-day audience – are 'dead language', telling only of old, forgotten, far-off things and battles long ago, they can be treated with the dispassionate philological objectivity to which Bakhtin refers.

In general, however, this is not the way that Bakhtin sees literary texts as operating. Literary texts – all texts – are for him as dialogic in origin as speech is: they are 'a verbal performance in print' (p. 95); they are constructed with an awareness of genre, the conventions of which they either obey or modify; they anticipate readerly reactions of various kinds. In fact, it would be interesting to construct a case that Bakhtin anticipated the Constance school in the notion of the virtual reader, and also anticipated speech act theory in general, though certainly not its narrow and restrictive view of literary utterances, in his assertion that the printed verbal performance 'responds to something, objects to something, affirms something . . . seeks support, and so on' (p. 95).

So, Bakhtin is saying, at point of origin the printed text is as dialogic and as ideological as any other speech act, whereas after several millennia of social change it may be inert and, in the most limiting sense of the term, merely a historical document of primarily philological interest. But what happens in between these two times? Do we have to suppose a series of discrete Saussurean synchronic systems, so to speak, each analytically distinct from others in the series? Or is there a process of gradual diachronic modification, during which the text first changes meaning and then loses it? Such questions have a particular force when we consider Bakhtin's insistence that 'Verbal communication can never be understood and explained outside of (a) connection with a concrete situation' (p. 95) and that it is 'always accompanied with social acts of a nonverbal character (the performance of labor, the symbolic acts of a ritual, a ceremony, etc.), and is often only an accessory to these acts' (p. 95). In the study of literary texts in classrooms, the first of these conditions is certainly met, and I want to go on to consider how far the second may be as well.

But first a clarification of terms. I have used 'meaning' above as an all-encompassing expression, but Bakhtin introduced an important differentiation between 'meaning' proper, by which he meant 'all those aspects of the utterance that are *reproducible* and *self-identical* in all instances of repetition' (p. 100) – the notion of the way in which an ideal dictionary would work in an idealized world can be helpful here – and 'theme', which is individual, unreproducible, and grounded in the immediate situation. Bakhtin's example of this was the utterance 'What time is it?', where the meaning remains constant, but the theme changes with the hands on the clock. Meaning is therefore a potentiality within a word which can be realized only within an utterance.

The corollary to meaning is understanding, and here Bakhtin distinguishes between passive understanding, such as is found in the philological response to ancient text, and the more typical active understanding, which involves response, participation in dialogue, and the matching of a speaker's word with a counter-word. It goes without saying that this latter is the more common type of activity undertaken by readers and speakers, and most of the interesting studies of class-room discourse in the past twenty years or so have concentrated their attentions on this type of speech activity.

The last third of Bakhtin's text deals with issues concerned with reported speech, and the final point I want to make in the course of this brief summary of the volume relates to this. Reported speech superficially appears a drily syntactic issue, but Bakhtin concentrates on it because it provides an 'objective document of . . . reception' (p. 117) which demonstrates the thoroughly social nature of the process.

> It is the function of society to select and to make grammatical (adapt to the gram-matical structure of its language) just those factors in the active and evaluative reception of utterances that are socially vital and constant, and, hence, that are grounded in the economic existence of the particular community of speakers. (p. 117)

What happens, therefore, in the production of reported speech is that two speech acts take place at once: a repetition of the original speech act in a suitably modified form, and a new speech act in which the current speaker adds his or her own inflections to the reported utterance. It is as though the original concept of dialogue – that of intersecting utterances originating in two different voices – has been collapsed inwards, so that the tension of word and counter-word is found now within the single utterance. This process is something that Bakhtin calls 'speech interference'.

And now, finally, I want to apply some of these terms and concepts to the lesson I described earlier. The pupils were lower sixth formers, aged seventeen or thereabouts, attending a state-maintained school, and they had just started to study Shakespeare's *Much Ado About Nothing*. An earlier lesson had done some initial scene-setting, but the teacher still had a lot that she wanted to do in establishing the social milieu in which the action of the play was to take place. In her comments to me subsequently she stressed that parts of the lesson were therefore more concerned with the transmission of information than she would consider normal for her. The pupils, nine of them, four boys and five girls, were gathered about six tables pushed together, and the teacher sat as one of their number, though from time to time she made her way to the blackboard to enter what she considered key terms on it; she was the only participant in the discussion to do this, although she pointed out to me afterwards that this was not always the case. The whole lesson lasted about forty-five minutes.

A microphone sat in the middle of the table, and I had made it clear that for that session all I proposed to do was to act as a recording engineer. All participants knew I was conducting some research into English teaching, but had no clear idea what this might consist of. My presence was undoubtedly a factor in the situation: the pupils commented afterwards that one of their number, usually vociferous, was silent, whereas another, Hashmat, spoke much more than normal. They did not, however, report feeling that what was said was wildly different from the normal tenor of their classroom discussion.

The choice of a Shakespeare text was a fortunate one from the perspective of this book, since it can be seen as falling on a scale somewhere between what Bakhtin would call the merely philological – as if, so to speak, the pupils were being trained to decode the Rosetta Stone – and some ultra-contemporary text which appeared to differ not at all from the pupils' own speech usages. In my 'Rosetta Stone' example, pupils would be required merely to decode the passage, to map out a series of dictionary meanings, to concentrate on the medium and not the message. In this lesson, however, it was clear that the teacher's attention was only to a limited degree focused on 'meaning' in Bakhtin's sense, and that she was chiefly concerned with what he would term 'theme'.

Two particular points might well strike the naïve observer who had never experienced the teaching of literature in schools. The first is that the purpose of the study of the play was, in general, treated as deeply implicit in the situation. The second is that, with relatively few exceptions, there was an absence of overt acknowledgement that this was a play at all – despite the fact that the style of the characters' discourse constituted the overt subject of the lesson. The naturalizing strategy of the teacher was mainly expressed by a concentration on the characters of Benedick and his companions, with a series of questions designed to elicit interpretation of motives. It is on these that I shall wish to focus shortly, but I want first to look at a passage which contains almost the only point in the lesson at which goals external to the lesson were explicitly mentioned.

The following is taken from a long introductory passage by the teacher very near the beginning of the lesson, and is punctuated by the squeak of chalk on board:

> OK. I was thinking about this last night, and I was thinking you did so much, honestly, you did so much good talking generally when we went through the first part of it in detail that sometimes you know when you're talking you can not take down really basic things. So I thought before we think about going a bit further on with the text I thought there were one or two things that I thought we should make sure we've got down in headings. Some of you if you are beginning to do your work in books then that might be a good thing to get it down but what I'm really concerned about is getting the vocabulary. I know you all wrote down all the good ideas that came but actually have we got the working vocabulary that came out of it which is (Pupil: Yes) the bit for me to do? So I thought, why don't we do this? I'll just shoot it up on the board quickly. Who were the specialists on the society? I mean some of you were and some of you weren't and we then developed fromwards [sic] ourselves.

If we take this passage at its face value, the teacher is praising the contributions of the pupils, listing the vocabulary that emerged from a previous discussion, and recognizing the particular, and relatively high-status, input of those who are 'specialists on the society'. She emphasized later that she regarded 'flattery' of this kind as an important teaching tool. In practice, though, rather different things are happening as well. The premature confirmation from a pupil that he has 'got the working vocabulary' is ignored; this is 'the bit for her to do'. It is clear that a particular set of terms is looked for, and it proves to be the case that the 'specialists' are not acknowledged or treated as such in the ensuing dialogue. I pick up a few seconds later. George is trying to describe Messina – the setting of the first scene.

George: Was it a rural sort of town away from [inaudible]?
Teacher: Rural – go on. You – you don't mean a village though do you?
George: No, no.
Teacher: But you don't mean a city?
George: Yeah.
Teacher: OK. So what we're talking about there is – the word for that is provincial, isn't it?
George: Yeah – or it's . . .
Teacher: It's a sort of smallish town. Mmm [pause]. I mean you established an awful lot, if I remember, about the society and the people and what you'd gathered.
Elaine: Aristocratic society.
Teacher: Certainly that was what we were consolved [sic] with. Yeah? [Pause] Come on – every now and again you get fed up with using the word aristocratic.
Jennifer: Behaviour, and the way to go about things.
A pupil: Yeah.
A pupil: Rank is important.
Teacher: Rank, Everybody.
George: Hierarchy.
Teacher: Good. Oh, somebody took some notes. Well done. Yes. Right. Rank, hierarchy. If you get some help – I mean, we are preparing for an exam now. This is a totally examined [pause] text that we're doing now. It's not the way we were before, so we do need something, so if you get fed up of writing aristocratic, another one that might do is patrician, or noble. All right? Yeah? So we've got a society that's very concerned with rank or hierarchy. I don't think we need to go through the reasons for that because we worked through it last time.

This is a long extract, and one that is rich in examples of the kind of issues I am addressing. To begin with, I would like to direct attention to the early part of it, and consider that contested use of the word 'rural'. George's utterance proposing it tails off into incoherence and inaudibility, and I am assuming – I'm afraid I wasn't quick enough to catch it – that he was receiving powerful non-verbal cues that his term was an inappropriate one. Earlier I quoted Bakhtin to the effect that verbal events are accompanied by others of a non-verbal character, and this holds good even in such a sedentary activity as an English lesson. But George's term seems not to be instantly dismissed – at least this is the case if we attend only to the meaning and ignore the theme. The teacher replies 'Rural – go on', and then, after the slightest of pauses, herself continues 'You – you don't mean a village though do you?'

Listening to the tape, I find it hard to decide whether she intended 'Go on' to be taken at face value or not; I think there was a change of gear during some tenths of a second. If 'Go on' was intended, though, it has the thematic force of something like 'Talk yourself out of this one', as the intonation makes very clear. Instead, though, she opts to set a limit on the scale of rurality – 'You don't mean a village.' George is happy to concur: 'No, no.' The teacher's response to this parallels, in its syntactic form, her previous utterance: 'But you don't mean a city?' Here she is setting an upper limit on the scale of rurality, and George's response accepts this limit also: 'Yeah.' But notice what we have here: two responses by George, accepting the teacher's categorizations, and therefore identical in theme, but in *meaning*, in Bakhtin's sense, the polar opposites to each other. The way I read this is that George's focus, in the first utterance, is on the content, which he is repudiating, whereas in the second he is concentrating on the maintenance of classroom cohesion, to which he is offering his assent.

The teacher's subsequent 'OK', as Sinclair and Coulthard (1975) would have pointed out, functions as the end of that particular micro-passage, which the teacher then establishes by her rather *ex cathedra* use of the word 'provincial', a term which it is reasonable to suppose she has had in her mind for some time. Indeed she confirmed to me that, like 'rank' and 'hierarchy', it was a term she intended to see brought into use. Unfortunately, however, George has not read his Sinclair and Coulthard, and he responds to the meaning of the tag at the end of the teacher's utterance – 'the word for that is provincial, isn't it?' – rather than to its theme, and attempts to offer what might, in his judgement, have proved to be an acceptable synonym or alternative formulation. The teacher's 'It's a sort of smallish town' therefore has two functions: it attempts to encapsulate what we might call the correction of course that has been achieved, and, with a different orientation, it successfully extinguishes George's attempted interpolation which would have been a threat to this course correction.

Throughout the portion of the interchange that I have been concentrating on, it may have seemed reasonable to suppose that the teacher's reality criteria – one aspect of what Bakhtin called the domain of ideology – are derived from the text of the play, so that the rural/urban characterization of Messina is judged in this light. Getting the word 'provincial' on to the board therefore has an importance that is derived from this source. However, as the lesson progresses it becomes clear that the question of vocabulary has other ideological reference points in addition to consideration of truth to the text. The section that I am thinking of here is the discussion of the type of society in which the characters in the play figure.

Elaine offers 'aristocratic society' as a definition. The response 'Certainly that was what we were consoled with' accepts it as adequate; the pronoun 'we' validates it on behalf of both the teacher and the group, but serves also to bracket the term off as something finished and done with, as opposed to what 'you' and 'I' are currently discussing. The involuntary portmanteau neologism arises, I would guess, because the teacher's attention is already directed towards alternatives. So issues attached to 'aristocratic' are not only something that 'we' were 'concerned' with, but also something that has been 'solved' or 'resolved'.

I invited the teacher to comment on the neologism; interestingly, her own response led off in a different direction, relating it to her previous experience of teaching different, older, age groups, and the difficulty she felt she experienced in deploying an appropriate lexicon in her teaching style.

After a pause the pupils are told 'Come on; after a while you get fed up with using the word "aristocratic".' All other uses of the pronoun 'you' in this passage relate to the pupils, either individually or collectively, and relate to activities that the pupils have in reality undertaken. This present usage is clearly of a different order; there is no evidence that the pupils are bored with the term, and the pronoun seems therefore, in Althusserian terms, much more like an interpellation, in which a role is created for the pupils whilst they are being summoned to occupy it. But whereas interpellation in Althusser is a serious matter, and by implication characterized usually by success, this interpellation has some of the features of a transparent rhetorical device, in which the pupils are invited to become aware of what it is about the role that they are being required to play.

So the word 'behaviour' is regarded as no solution to the problem of hypothetical boredom, although it is endorsed by one other voice in the room, whereas 'rank' and 'hierarchy' are clearly seen as acceptable. There then follows an utterance to which the printed page fails utterly to do any justice. 'Oh, somebody took some notes. Well done. Yes.' As set down in type, this indicates simple approval. The intonation of the utterance, however, is heavy with irony, which appears to distance the value of note-taking from both speaker and hearers. This is still not it, however, since the ironic utterance is actually being used as a vehicle for a much convoluted form of approval.

Why is this extraordinary speech performance necessary? If we look at the context in the transcript, we see that the teacher is working round to presenting the terms 'patrician' and 'noble' as acceptable stylistic variants of 'aristocratic'. 'Stylistic' in Bakhtin tends to indicate something that may have originated in an individual speech performance, but has then become codified either within similar discourses, or, more rarely, within the structure of the language itself. In terms of this particular dialogue, these two new terms do originate with the teacher, but she explicitly relates their appropriateness to the whole apparatus of public examinations. The notion that the pupils might get 'fed up' with the original term is in many ways akin to the 'transparent interpellation' that I referred to earlier. There is perhaps then a certain irony in the choice not to go into the reasons why a society is not concerned with rank and hierarchy, that only becomes apparent when the transcript of the lesson is examined in this way.

Note-taking is therefore akin to the possession of an appropriate vocabulary, in that it is seen by the teacher as the product of powerful external constraints, which it is her responsibility to mediate, but from which she therefore wishes in some way to differentiate herself. The pause in 'this is a totally examined – text' is, I should judge, the longest that occurs in any of her quasi-monologic utterances; it does not correspond to any solicitation of an answer, and it does not seem to occur to any of the pupils to interrupt it. Why does it occur? It may well have been a response to my presence; perhaps I held views on examinations and how to prepare for them. More probably, however, it corresponds to some rapid passage of inner speech which runs through, in an only half-articulated way, the constraints that are in play. Subsequently, indeed, she stressed to me her experience of working for examining boards, and the strong belief she derived from that activity in the necessity for candidates to exhibit a rich and appropriate vocabulary.

I want now to turn to another segment of the lesson, and to another set of Bakhtin's terms that I introduced earlier. This is the distinction between the philological response to dead text, concerned solely with meaning of a dictionary kind, and dialogic response to 'live' utterance, in which word is matched with counter-word.

Each pupil in the classroom had his or her own copy of the play, but a variety of editions was being used. The teacher proposed to have a segment of text read aloud. She directed attention to Act 1, Scene 1, line 146, and then said:

> Now can I leave it to you, if there's anything desperate that you don't understand, you will ask, won't you? I don't feel that we'll have to go through every single little word; on the other hand we've all got different, slightly different books, so if you find there's anything interesting in your book that you think would be worthwhile offering to somebody else, because the Arden ones are very worth – have got interesting footnotes, haven't they, do do do put it in as usual – OK?

I am assuming that 'interesting' here implies philologically interesting, and that the teacher is indicating a concern with meaning rather than with theme. During this and subsequent occasions when pupils read text aloud, no one took up the offer to comment on meaning in this way. On this occasion, at least, philological matters seemed of limited interest to them. 'Interesting' is, however, a key signal in the teacher's vocabulary – I must be careful with terms here, as Bakhtin would have us call it a sign – and I think the pupils are well-primed to respond to it, as other uses exemplify. Her remark to me subsequently was that she actually found the textual apparatus of the Arden edition necessary but boring.

Most of the time, however, attention is directed to theme within the text, as the following passage illustrates. I should emphasize that this passage is quoted here as being typical of the greater part of the lesson; in particular, we can notice here the greater proportion of talk sustained by the pupils. The lesson is now exploring the dominant themes of the society that is being studied: war and courtship have been agreed, and Beatrice has been established as rebellious and deviant in her character and in her interests.

John: They, she's – em, she doesn't fall for any doctrine and because she's arrogant, see, the blokes they say, oh look she – this ridiculous and that's why they're interested in her. Cos if all the women are the same you know it's your same old story you know you can ma – you just go up to her now and marry her but when there's somebody different who's hard to get as Benedick finds out you know he gets more interested.

Teacher: So we got Beatrice as unconventional. Now you're saying she's – no, you said she's arrogant, she's cynical, at this early stage, she's got plenty to say for herself. Where is her viewpoint got like? You say she's always got plenty to say for herself; why?

Hashmat: Is it because she was engaged she realized that men are dominant in her society and she can't [inaudible] she takes it but she doesn't want it that way.

Teacher: Doesn't Hero realize that?

Hashmat: I think she does but Hero's more controlled by her father and therefore su-suppressed.

Within the conventions of classroom discussion a number of different sub-genres are being deployed. When John is talking about 'just going up to women and marrying one of them', we can assume that he is not generalizing from his own experience (at least as far as marriage is concerned) but imaginatively projecting himself into the world of Messina as he apprehends it. However, his vocabulary, with its use of terms such as 'blokes' and 'hard to get' is establishing a correspondence with his own society; he is naturalizing some of the values. What we have here is 'interference', not simply at the level of vocabulary or syntax, but also at the level of values.

The teacher and Hashmat have in common a more overtly analytical style of comment; the teacher continues to list key terms, though not all she lists have been offered by pupils. Both Hashmat and she appear to be in sympathy with 'unconventionality' as it is manifested by both Beatrice and Benedick. However, the teacher's attitudes are more ambiguous than they at first appear. A pupil uses the word 'professed' in relation to Benedick's expression of his views.

Teacher: That word 'professed' therefore – what is that saying about his role in society; what do the rest of these people do to him? Isn't there a sense there that they always expect him to have something to say, and they always expect him to be the one with the cle-clever, witty statement? Have you ever I mean did you ever see that in your lower schools I mean teachers are always aware that sometimes a kid gets clobbered with being the class wit, you know, and everybody relies on them you know they're probably getting a bit bored aren't they and everybody wants the subject changed so it's somebody who they think 'Right, he can do it' and and that's something that teachers are always aware of and maybe when you get to know them as people they don't want to play this role. They were like that in the first second and third year and then they really want to

> work terribly hard and they want to get their exams but they're lumbered
> with this role of being what everybody expects them to be you know the
> class fool or the class entertainer and I just wonder if there there is
> Benedick's sense of he knows that people use him because he's entertain-
> ing and because he's funny. And there is a double statement there.

There is indeed. The use of a word such as 'clobbered' throws out a line
towards the register in which, for example, John was operating a few minutes
earlier. The most powerful reference backwards, though, is towards the notion
of adjusting your vocabulary to the demands of the examination. Just as these
pupils will have to discuss the play using an appropriate vocabulary, so Benedick
has to conform to the social expectations of Messina – just as a bright, comical,
naughty pupil has to learn that he really wants to be a good, hardworking
sixth-former. Thus the structure and texture of the play provide a powerful vali-
dation of the functioning of the school, despite the apparent charms of the
'unconventionality' of Beatrice and Benedick. The use of the pronoun system is,
as usual, most significant. 'You' refers originally to the experience of being a
lower school pupil. But in 'when you get to know them as people' the referent
has changed to a teacher, and the passage as a whole shifts viewpoint from that
of the peer group to that of the staffroom, though the concluding 'you know'
implicates the present audience in the classroom in this shift as well. As such it
can be taken to be successful; the pupils, when invited to comment on this passage, spent some time explaining that during their previous education they had
indeed known several pupils of whom this was an accurate description.

The last excerpt I want to take from this phase of the lesson relates to a line
spoken by Benedick to Claudio:

> *Teacher:* So, what about Benedick's statement 'Would you buy her that you
> enquire after her?' [Pause] What are the implications that Benedick is
> perhaps suggesting there? [Repeats line]
>
> *Hashmat:* Is it prostitution?
>
> *Henry:* It's like he's he's trying to tell him that it's not love that you feel, it's
> conventions again. It's em you know you got to do the right thing sort
> of thing So I mean he's only just seen her doesn't know anything about
> her so when he says 'Would you buy her?' it's very much like buying
> something.
>
> *Teacher:* So what's that – so what are the implications below that statement then
> about what Benedick feels about courtship? I mean maybe we're work-
> ing too deeply at that bit now but you know what we do what we set
> ourselves up and then we break them down the rest of the play.

As in a previous excerpt, in which Hashmat hazarded a guess at paternal
suppression, the more radical comment-cum-interpretation that she is offering
here is not taken up, whereas it is Henry's comment, which first refers back to
the approved topic of conventions, and ends on a tautology, that secures a
response. Having failed to elicit a response from the teacher, Hashmat then has a
second attempt, offering a less radical comparison with something that you buy

from a shop, like a jumper, and then reject. 'Well, that's the implication, isn't it, that these are goods on display in a shop', the teacher confirms; she then takes the conversation in another direction, and no overt evaluation of the simile is subsequently provided.

The pupils subsequently had a good deal to say about Hashmat's contributions; she herself chanced to be absent during this ensuing session. Drawing on her remarks earlier in the year, they commented that, whereas she was an ardent advocate of women's rights, she nevertheless supported the practice of arranged marriages. To them this appeared a contradiction; her account, however, had centred on the unreliability of romance as the basis of a relationship.

Later in the lesson – and this is the final piece of transcript that I want to examine here – the question of why Benedick makes the comments he does to Claudio is returned to once again. Henry suggests that this is done to dissuade Claudio from marriage, and concludes:

Henry: . . . A joke with the lads sort of thing, so perhaps he's trying to lead him along into saying no to Hero so to keep him friendly.

Teacher: To keep the gang together.

George: Beer partner [general laughter].

Teacher: That's right, yes. So they can all go out drinking on Saturday evenings as opposed to [inaudible interruption] instead of taking the girl to the cinema yes. And just when the situation that's an interesting point there because another member of the boy gang comes along: 'enter Don Pedro'.

Here, I think, we can see several things happening at once. There is certainly a kind of language interference, as the process of male bonding in the play is transposed into a present-day analogy. Noteworthy, too, is the participation of the teacher in the construction of this analogy – no ifs or buts here – as opposed to her reluctance to enter into any comparable process in respect of suggestions of suppression of women by fathers, or of the marriage market as analogous to prostitution. There are slight but observable generational and cultural differences: I cannot see the teacher referring to a beer partner, or the boys thinking quite so immediately of a visit to the cinema, but these are trivial in comparison to the general air of collusion. So, although the teacher has made much play throughout the lesson with notions such as 'conventional' in a distancing kind of way, I cannot see that in the end she detaches herself significantly from the conventions prevalent in the depiction of Messina, or from the image of it that the male pupils have constructed.

In discussing this section of the lesson, the teacher pointed out that it was unusual to have so high a proportion of boys in a sixth-form English set – she gave a graphic and amusing description of feeling as if the windows were darkened when the students stood up during their first lesson together – but gave no indication of being aware of responding more to their contributions than to those of the girls. She stressed that a very vocal girl was absent on that day, and offered the interesting comment that she saw that girl as 'another Beatrice' and one of the boys as having a similar resemblance in character to Benedick. Despite the care that is taken to characterize the society of Messina, it is clear that she does not see it as altogether alien.

Let me emphasize that I am not, in this book, concerned with the question of whether the lesson generated a fair or accurate interpretation of *Much Ado about Nothing*; for my present purposes, it is enough to point out that it is a complex and ambiguous text from which the activity of the lesson has overtly extracted one set of meanings whilst leaving other possibilities attenuated or unexplored. The actual practices of the lesson – the distribution of turns between teacher and pupil, and between boys and girls, and the differing receptions accorded to these latter – do more than parallel the reading of the play; they are instrumental in its creation and maintenance.

Since this is a conclusion towards which I have been working for some little time, it might well be expected that I should now say that this is how a prevailing ideology, generated a long way from this particular classroom, gets into the heads of school pupils, or at any rate how it is reinforced. This is not quite how I should wish to put it, and, just as I used Bakhtin in the first half of this chapter, I now want to return to Foucault for assistance in explaining what may be going on here in relation to the creation and distribution of power.

In a series of books, Foucault looked at the creation of a series of carceral institutions – prisons, hospitals, and mental asylums. Schools also figured in his list, though they never received from him the kind of extensive examination that he devoted to the other institutions I have listed. They belong with them, though, in that their widespread development is a post-Enlightenment phenomenon, and Foucault was concerned to pull the rug from under our conception of the benevolence of these developments.

Schools resemble prisons and hospitals in the rigorously organized use of space, and in the development of a series of practices ostensibly dedicated to the individualization and improvement of their inmates. They resemble psychotherapy or confession in their use of the 'talking cure' to bring about their desired results. Like the other all-enveloping institutions listed here, they function through the deployment of power. 'Power', though, for Foucault, has a very specific meaning, and it is important to establish just what this is.

When Bakhtin speaks of ideology, he uses it, on occasion though by no means invariably, in the classic Marxist sense of a complex of ideational and behavioural norms that cause members of one class to opt to act in ways that are conducive to the advantage of another class. In Foucault's terms, this is domination rather than power, since such an ideology is fully in tune with the interests of the dominant class, and this class can both logically and temporally precede the start of such domination. In contrast, it has often been observed, from a more phenomenological perspective, that gaolers are locked up during their shift just as much as prisoners are – indeed, they can't *be* gaolers until this happens – and many teachers have experienced a comparable sensation on entering the classroom. Foucault's way of putting this is to say that the exercise of power simultaneously creates both the exerciser and the recipient of the activity. In his discussion of Bentham's Panopticon, referred to in the previous chapter, he demonstrated the way in which the regime simultaneously and from point of origin controls and directs both inmates and warders, very much, to use a homely analogy, as the rudimentary barometer works both Jack and Jill in the weather-house; their motions are different, but reciprocal.

In the first volume of *The History of Sexuality* (1980b), Foucault wrote: 'power is not an institution, and not a structure; neither is it a certain strength we are endowed with; it is the name that one attributes to a complex strategical relationship in a particular society' (p. 93). It is a series of historical forces and directions, involving and drawing sustenance from individual will and fore-thought, but totally beyond the control and direction of any individual or group.

Such a conception of power is open to the charge of mystification, and such charges have indeed been laid. However, it seems to me that it is helpful to us, whatever its larger strengths and weaknesses, in looking at what gets done during classroom discourse, and at the way in which it involves both teacher and pupils in an only sometimes unwitting and unintended collusion, the outcome of which affects both parties.

'Power', says Foucault, 'comes from below', and in the passages we have been looking at, and especially the last one, it seems to me that it is often the pupils as well as the teacher who are calling the tune. She has introduced the text, and the text has passages relating to male bonding and the subordinate role of women, but the reference to 'beer partners' is not hers, it is something that meets general approval, and it is something that the logic of her presentation causes her to accept. In contrast, Hashmat's attempts to secure attention for the role of the dominant father, or for the resemblance of marriage to prostitution, constitute what Foucault would term resistance, which, in the specific sense of the term discussed earlier, is a frequent, perhaps even invariable, accompaniment to the exercise of power.

In my use of Foucault here I am not seeking to deny the existence of larger social formations or pressures; I am drawing on the privileges of eclecticism, and it was Bakhtin who described the eclectic as blithe. Certainly it is impossible to ignore the fact that the apparatus of the 'A' level exam exists, for instance: examiners sit in panelled rooms and set questions. And behind them are other levers of political machinery, including Kenneth Baker's rejection, as Secretary of State for Education, of the proposals for the reform of the sixth-form exam-ination system contained in the Higginson Report, and indeed the later 1991 White Paper. But that whole apparatus of domination gets into this classroom through the teacher's construction of it, and I would suggest that the compiling of acceptable vocabulary lists is her initiative and not the Board's. When scripts come to be marked, however, the use of such lists will be an observable reality, and an outcome of the deployment of power. In the same way, the dominance of patriarchy existed before the beginning of this lesson, and the lesson both reflects and refracts this phenomenon, but it also to a degree creates it, even whilst it offers a demonstration of this process against which resistance can shove.

The attraction of such an interpretation of what is going on is that it does not have to deny participants all awareness of their actions, or of the consequences of their actions, even if it absolves them of complicity in the furthest reaches of their implications. It was Foucault who put this point most neatly: 'People know what they do; they frequently know why they do what they do; but what they don't know is what what they do does' (cited in Dreyfus and Rabinow, 1982:187).

4 Nationalizing the English curriculum

A significant part of this book so far has dealt with the traditions and assumptions within English teaching that date from the 1960s and 1970s. This does not mean that they are not in general use today, for mental furniture, like the upholstered kind, has a general tendency to continue in service until it falls to bits and is replaced by something else. Change can, however, be rapid as well as gradual, and the succession of Education Acts in the 1980s, and particularly in the second half of the decade, is precipitating in the 1990s a major shift in educational attitudes as well as in educational provision.

This is not to imply, however, that there is a simple and immediate congruence between educational legislation and professional culture. Indeed, for a good part of this century it could be argued that the opposite has been the case. During the 1930s, when secondary education was available only to those individuals who could afford it, and to a selected minority who could obtain scholarships, the prevailing model does indeed appear to have been, as Dixon argued, that of the cultural heritage, with its heavily corporatist implications. In the post-war period of educational consensus which succeeded the 1944 Education Act, however, when equality, however variously defined, was the keyword, and notions of statist and communal responsibility for the provision of education for all were not automatically derided, the prevailing model was clearly that of personal growth. In terms of abstract logic, though, it is in some ways easier to equate the personal growth model with the privatization of education that is to be found in and around the 1988 Education Act. Both, for instance, can be seen as premissed upon an atomistic view of the individual, whose needs and aspirations can be satisfied by an educational programme which is, or at least appears, tailor-made rather than mass-produced. In the case of English teaching, this is achieved by a rich and enabling literary and linguistic environment which enables psychological and educational development to take place at the maximum rate. In the case of school selection, the implied promise is that we shall see a proliferation of types of school – maintained, grant-aided, grant-maintained, direct grant, city technology college, independent, grammar, perhaps even secondary modern – from which the individual consumer can select.

This comparison between the pedagogical model and recent legislation is of course in all sorts of ways misleading. For one thing, the personal growth model was typically sustained in practice by a variety of implicit assumptions which saw society and community as beneficial features of the learning environment; constraints, if you like, but also resources, and as such acceptable and indeed welcome features of any educational setting. More specifically, the rich learning environment was implicitly seen as the outcome of a sufficiency of public investment in the educational process. Contrariwise, the notion of an open and free choice of school is in practice counteracted by varying parental abilities to provide fees and travel costs, and, more radically again, by varying parental access to information upon which rational choice can be based. As Lynch puts it (1989, p. 33), 'there is no reason for the wise to inform the innocent'.

The major internal contradiction in recent legislation, though, is, as Whitty (1990) points out, that changes in the structure of school provision are ostensibly designed to maximize parental choice as regards types of educational provision, whilst at the same time the establishment of the national curriculum (at least in respect of those schools sufficiently within the maintained orbit to be controlled by it) clearly restricts it. Whitty shows how it is possible to equate commitment to parental choice of school with the neo-liberal strand within New Right thinking, and control over the curriculum with the neo-conservative element within it. He then considers to what degree New Right thinking can reconcile these two, logically contradictory, strands. In this I suspect he is possibly being unnecessarily scrupulous; the history of right-wing administrations in Europe during this century suggests that they are more adept than left-wing ones in not letting unresolved contradictions at the level of ideology interfere with the business of government. Indeed, Johnson (1991) persuasively argues that neo-liberalism and neo-conservatism need each other. But, in a sense, this is precisely Whitty's point, since he later considers the possibility that state control over the curriculum (particularly in respect of those schools most potentially oppositionist in nature) represents a short-term goal by legislating dissent out of existence, whilst a full-blown policy of privatization and reliance upon the workings of the market is intended, in the long term, to sweep away oppositionist schools in any case. If I can contribute an analogy of my own at this point, New Right thinking on this issue can be seen as a mirror image of the development of state socialism in the USSR in the 1920s, with privatization as the equivalent to the long-term goal of communism, and the National Curriculum as the equivalent of the New Economic Plan. Just as the NEP was intended to use capitalist methods to speed up the early phases of the development of a socialist society, so Whitty sees the implementation of the National Curriculum as a communalist tactic that is subordinated to the individualistic strategy of a privatized educational system.

Neo-liberalism and neo-conservatism potentially differ also in their attitudes towards the demands that industry makes of education provision for the future workforce. The neo-conservative hostility towards 'relevance' as a criterion for the selection of educational material is primarily directed at pedagogies such as that of personal growth, but logically it encompasses also the notion of specific training for future industrial employment. Neo-liberalism, on the contrary, welcomes the notion of relevance of this latter kind, and it is neo-liberal thinking which has led to the recruitment of large numbers of local industrialists to the governing bodies of schools under the provisions of the 1986 Act. Henceforward such people will no longer have to have their views mediated by a contemporary equivalent of the Newbolt Committee; they will be in a position to express themselves directly in an arena in which curriculum policy is determined.

Moreover, it is apposite to mention that industrialists have already had an opportunity to control the curriculum even more directly; the invitation that successive Secretaries of State for Education have extended to them to finance city technology colleges, whose curriculum and ethos can then be constructed around their own predilictions and preferences, has however received a very tepid response. This has resulted in the entertaining irony of Treasury money being dedicated in significant quantities to the establishment of such schools; we are entitled to wonder what a Treasury ethos would look like if that august institution took its role as patron of the curriculum to its logical conclusion. Furthermore, the pattern of relatively high wastage of appointees from governing bodies, as the extent of the demands upon voluntary input of time to meet the needs of Local Management of Schools becomes gradually apparent, may also come to erode industrial management's contribution of personnel to the management of the curriculum on a month-by-month basis.

Nevertheless, at a national level at least, and probably to a considerable extent at a local level as well, it is to be expected that the contribution of industrial management to the formulation of curriculum policy will be considerable. What remains to be seen, therefore, is whether, in respect of English teaching, this will lead to an emphasis on 'skills' in what we can now call the historic sense (broadly speaking, reading and writing) or whether the more recent notion of the acquisition of transferable skills will prevail.

If skills in the historic sense should win, then industrial management will find itself aligned with neo-conservatives in their emphasis on 'standards', and with that not inconsiderable proportion of those parents involved in the business of school selection whose criteria for choice are based on a reconstruction of an idealized version of their own education. If, as I think more likely, notions of transferable skills prove to be dominant, then it is possible that industry may come to look more favourably on a suitably adapted version of the personal growth model, with its emphasis on life skills. In this latter case, there is some possibility that they will be able to carry elements from within the neo-liberal camp with them.

One aspect of this issue has already surfaced in the requirement that five per cent of GCSE marks should be vulnerable to deduction in order to penalize persistent bad spelling, or misspelling of key terms. This requirement, it should be noted, applies right across the curriculum, and is not confined to English, though one aspect of the rhetoric deployed relates bad spelling to progressive, child-centred teaching styles in this subject. Since it can be argued that this attention to presentation can only be improved at the expense of time spent on the teaching of substantive subject content, it seems probable that the regulation is to be counted as a victory for the neo-conservatives. The key question for industrialists, therefore, is whether, either out of conviction or for more ideologically-related reasons, they support a concentration on spelling during the years of GCSE teaching, or whether they would prefer to see more substantive teaching taking place, and rely on their future employees running spelling-checking programmes on their word-processors in due course.

To the extent that the above comments relate to English as a school subject, they deal with the 'language' element of English as a core component of the national curriculum. As far as literature is concerned, its options seem in many ways more restricted. As is well known, the diminution of a separate examination subject titled 'Literature' is a departure from the practice of the GCE, and can only serve to marginalize the contribution of 'literature' to 'English' generally. Yet the National Curriculum, taken as an entity, is a deeply conservative concept in its emphasis on traditional school subjects within traditional subject boundaries. To that extent, inertia may be said to favour the continuation of a literature element within the subject, even if the specific arguments about its benefits once adduced by Newbolt are now regarded as highly specious. The logic of this therefore points towards a revivified, if limited, version of the cultural heritage model to which Newbolt was wedded, and it is this aspect that, appropriately enough, holds most appeal for neo-conservatives. Indeed, with the revival of narrative verse on historical subjects receiving the attention of no less a person than Kenneth Baker during his time as Secretary of State for Education, we have even witnessed tentative moves to rescind the earlier divorce between history and English.

To some degree, however, both neo-liberals and neo-conservatives share a potential interest in a cultural heritage model. Neo-conservatives have a strong stake in the inculcation of a Burkean belief in the role of the state as the repository of shared traditions and values. Within the history curriculum, for example, this is evidenced by the strong pressure towards a concentration on British political history which, if contextualized at all, is to be seen within a highly Eurocentric universe. The same impulse which, in its negative form, opposes anti-racist programmes and multicultural education is also likely to adopt a positive attitude towards any material which develops a belief in a monocultural nation state. There is not the same intrinsic opposition on the part of neo-liberals to the notion of multiculturalism, or the same gut commitment to the nation state as such, but they do retain a belief in the necessity for some form of regulatory body to hold the ring, to see that the markets are allowed to work in an unrestrained fashion, and to administer correction to those who attempt to obstruct this process. The nation state as currently known best serves these ends,

and action which is taken to sustain it is likely to be at least weakly supported –
provided it does not require too large a slice of the timetable.

This last point is likely to be crucial, since pressure generated by the National
Curriculum is already intense, and future developments are likely to increase
rather than reduce this pressure. In particular, I am thinking here of the
combined effects, through the next decade and more, of two factors. The first is
a likely shortage of employees as a result of a demographic drop. The second is a
belated recognition of an enormous shortfall in the proportion of young people
undertaking any form of education after the age of sixteen. Though the immediate consequences of this as set out in the 1991 White Paper are those that will
affect colleges, polytechnics, and universities, there will inevitably be a backwash
into schools once they are required to provide what will amount to 'access'
courses for post-sixteen education and training. As far as 'English' is concerned
(and the inverted commas are meant to imply that the whole content area must
henceforward be treated as problematic) the likeliest feature of this pressure will
be a demand for a greater level of engagement with a whole variety of aspects
of communication studies, and in particular those that have close vocational
relevance to the needs of commerce and industry as they are generally perceived.

All this is speculation about education at the end of the millennium. There
are, however, likely to be a number of changes before then arising out of the
distinction between schools which are required to offer the national curriculum
and those which are not. Whitty (1990:32) cites Shipman's (1980) comment that
trendy teachers experiment on other people's children while exposing their own
to the most traditional curriculum imaginable; his final conclusion is that:

> We should be thankful that the National Curriculum is there as the one remaining
> symbol of a common education system and specifiable entitlement which people
> can struggle collectively to improve, rather than letting all provision emerge from
> the individual exercise of choice (or non-choice) in the market-place. (p. 34)

It is however possible to speculate that Shipman's description may need to
be inverted, if articulate and informed middle-class parents, especially perhaps
those involved in National Curriculum-governed education themselves, increasingly opt for schools towards the 'independent' end of the spectrum of control
in order to secure for their children the benefits of a liberal education – perhaps
even sometimes of a pupil-centred variety. The approach to the teaching of
English adopted by various schools would then be a litmus test for attitudes to
the curriculum generally. In the kind of case I have outlined here, the parents'
attitude towards the National Curriculum, once they and their children were
freed from its direct consequences, would increasingly be a mixture of lip-service
and a kind of missionary concern; I recall, and feel tempted to update, the quip
of thirty years ago that Conservatives are people who would fight to the death for
the right of other people's children to go to grammar schools.

Nevertheless, it is seemingly inevitable that the National Curriculum will
become an area of contestation; the New Right is after all convinced that the

introduction of the GCSE examination was hijacked by those with a vested interest in the production, as opposed to the consumption, of education, and assessment is, amongst other things, intended to be a consumers' guide – or perhaps a kind of annual report to shareholders – and a safeguard against the same fate befalling this later and major innovation. The kind of information that an ideal form of assessment generates is capable of assisting and informing consumer choice – for those who have access to such information, that is. It may well be that the indirect effects of assessment, rather than the National Curriculum *per se*, will draw a significant number of schools from amongst those exempt from the requirements of the latter to adopt many of its features on a voluntary basis. But, though I can see how the sum of individual consumer decisions may bring about changes in the practice and adoption of the National Curriculum, I find it hard to be optimistic about the possibility of the kind of collective struggle that Whitty envisages, however democratic and admirable may be the impulse to applaud it. The analogy with the National Health Service may be an appropriate one here; public opinion surveys consistently show a high degree of public concern about the level of funding and the efficacy of provision, but public pressure does not begin to engage systematically with questions concerning the deployment of resources and the generation of priorities within the Service itself. Reluctantly, therefore, I conclude that the contest for the National Curriculum is likely to be fought out by the familiar armies from any number of previous educational campaigns: politicians, both national and local; teacher unions; DES and HMI; employers; universities, polytechnics and colleges in general as educators of school leavers; teacher educators as a particular interest group.

One other contrast with the National Health Service may be appropriate at this point, and one comparison as well. As Murphy (1990:39) has pointed out, testing as a form of market indicator is only appropriate if there is general agreement on what it is that is being tested. The Financial Times Index or the Dow Jones perfectly express the value of shares at a particular place and time. However, there is every reason to suppose that the pattern of national assessment as originally envisaged by the government possessed the virtues of political attractiveness and a kind of ascribed objectivity and rigour, rather than those of relevance to the full range of skills and knowledge that the National Curriculum sought to inculcate. Yet shortly afterwards the implications of what was actually envisaged began to become apparent, and teachers and others were forced to address the question of how testing would leave time for sufficient prior teaching to take place at all. A series of scaling-down exercises then ensued. This is not yet complete, and its total consequences remain imponderable, as does the degree to which it will impress the 'education-buying' public. Thus while, for the lay person at least, there exists some common-sense notion of what good health is, and therefore in principle some rough means of determining whether or not particular hospitals are successful in restoring patients to it, it remains to be seen whether the apparatus of levels as proposed by the Task Group on

Assessment and Testing, or the Standard Assessment Tasks, will be perceived by the school-selecting public as adequate market indicators.

But the better way (at least in terms of strict logic) in which market indicators can be used to evaluate an institution is to compare inputs and outputs, as Murphy (1990:38) reminds us. His point is that a school which takes children with multiple disadvantages and educates them to a reasonable standard is more efficient than one which secures slightly better absolute results for a much more advantaged group. This is true and important – but against it must be set the fact that many parents would consider they were making a rational choice to send their children to the second school rather than the first. Here a comparison with the Health Service (as it existed till recent changes in the direction of ostensibly greater consumer choice) again becomes appropriate. A hospital with a good record of treating childhood leukaemia might earn itself bonus points on a scale of merit – but parents might not choose to move to its catchment area if they found that it served Sellafield.

In the preceding paragraphs I have tried to map out something of the general context that the National Curriculum, and the evolution of plans for testing, provide for the teaching of English within schools. What I want to do now is to look at some of the ways in which, within an English Department in a school, teaching approaches are developed and advanced towards a degree of explicitness. I then want to look at some of the ways in which legislation to amend the provisions for the government of schools can have a bearing on this process.

A departmental approach based on the model of personal growth frequently, if not necessarily, assumed a high degree of teacher autonomy within the bounds of the classroom. At a minimal level, there would of course have to be co-ordination of the transfer of books and other teaching materials between classes at the end of term, agreement on the options to be selected for public examinations, and so on. However, what went on within each lesson was not subject to anything like the same degree of control, and indeed the tradition of the independence of the teacher in the classroom, inherited, paradoxically as it may seem, from much more overtly authoritarian styles of teaching, had the capacity to underwrite the more pupil-centred styles of teaching that were now being practised. As with much else in the educational system, rigorous control over entry to a particular selected group (in this case, people deemed qualified to teach, and, in most cases, to teach that particular subject) was coupled with a high degree of permissiveness with respect to what members of that group did afterwards.

Moreover, the way in which the pacing of the learning process was carried out meant that it was in any case difficult to prescribe particular learning outcomes at a particular stage in time. If the study of English was envisaged as a co-operative project to develop individual sensibilities, then pupils would properly be expected to advance at different rates over a given period of time. More importantly, it could be argued that the most valuable aspects of that development were the ones least available to outside inspection, and the ones where variability was most marked, since, within the bounds of the definition, it could hardly be alleged that there was a single common goal. It could even be suggested that significant growth and development could be expected of the teacher as well as of the pupils, if the teaching process was as authentically interactive as it was held to be.

The situation outlined above could be conducive both to professional autonomy and to feelings of anomie that could range from the mild to the acute. Partly, no doubt, to avoid the latter, English developed one of the more effective subject networks within the teaching profession. Indeed, it seems likely that many people would have found it difficult to engage in an activity with so few objectively demonstrable outcomes if they were not sustained by a reference group of some significance and standing. If a teacher was working in a department of like-minded colleagues, these would typically form the most immediate resource of this nature. If, however, the department consisted of a more disparate group of people, then supportive contact within a professional association would be correspondingly important.

In addition, although I have stressed the autonomy of the teacher, there were various aspects of common practice that served to diminish its more extreme manifestations. Team teaching might be employed in certain instances. Even when it was not, various schemes might be adopted for the sharing of teacher-generated material, ranging from the occasional exchange of master copies of worksheets to a fully funded and staffed resources centre. Such sharing might take place within a given school, or within a geographical area. In the latter case, the exchange might take place on the premises of a teachers' centre; the number of such institutions increased dramatically during the 1960s and 1970s. The growth in the number of LEA subject specialist advisers during the same period could also contribute to networking in various ways. Finally, the use that was made of in-service training resources during this time, although it varied greatly from employer to employer, might also serve to reinforce the self-image of teachers committed to a personal growth approach, either by sending a selected few on long courses to teacher training establishments, or by importing guest speakers to evening meetings; their prestige, in addition to whatever they might have to say, would help to confirm the teachers in their approach.

To recount the changes in resourcing which have limited or removed the support offered by these various sources would merely be depressing. It may be better, instead, to focus on the effect that the National Curriculum is having, and is likely to have, on various aspects of the professional culture. At the most naïvely optimistic interpretation, of course, it removes the necessity for doubt and self-questioning, and the opportunity for anomie; after all, if the subject is granted a central place in the overall curriculum, if its content and its subject method are specified in some detail, and if the performance of the teacher is ratified at various stages by the deployment of a national system of assessment, then people know exactly where they are.

I have indicated, in this and other chapters, various reasons that cause me to suppose it will not all happen like this. Even if the professional culture does not immediately cause teachers to 'teach for the exam', or, in this case, for assessment, mediated pressure from parents and others may well fairly rapidly impel teachers to adopt this as a goal. And yet just what 'teaching for assessment' would consist of remains unclear, as does the definition of the core element in this core subject. In such an ideologically riven area, it is just not possible for a National Curriculum document to state plainly and categorically what the subject is all about. It is not even possible that, as is the case with the history curriculum, there can be a public argument in which clear and opposed positions on this question are explicitly laid out.

If in the end, then, the subject is still a mystery wrapped in an enigma, the directed nature of the teacher's work is not accompanied by a sufficiently clear sense of where it is being directed towards. Whether this is a more confusing experience for the teacher trained in the subject, or for those whose induction has been more sudden and less structured, is difficult to say.

5 In search of a subject

In Chapter 3 I drew attention to the fact that, though a play was being studied in a classroom, there seemed to be no discussion either of the fact that it *was* a play (as opposed to, say, a transcript of actual recorded speech between Elizabethan or Italian courtiers) or of the purposes behind the institutionally-organized study of either composed or recorded dialogue. Of course such discussions may well have formed the substance of other lessons, either before or afterwards, and of course we all bring certain expectations to bear on the transaction we label as the study of literature in schools, whether we speak them aloud or not. But, as is so often the case, it is the unspoken assumptions which can tell us most about what is going on.

Consider again Foucault's three terms: capacity, communication, power. Shorn of the theoretical context, the first of these at least would have no problem in securing general assent as a desirable goal at even the most refractory parents' meeting or staff discussion; there is an almost universal commonsensical agreement that pupils go to school to learn how to do things, and that this learning involves planning and designing, as well as the ensuing physical activity. Bizarrely enough, Foucault's highly theoretical definition of the process occasionally comes to resemble the rationale offered for the universal adoption of CDT as a school subject. Communication would receive almost equal assent if portrayed in the traditional terms of learning to read and write, and more recent accretions such as the importance of skills in oracy might well be argued into the frame. Power might initially be perceived as belonging to a different universe of discourse, but could in the end perhaps be naturalized as the learning of a proper respect for others, and as the basis for self-discipline.

But of course the point about Foucault's tripartite classification is that it refers to the unspoken assumptions and unacknowledged activities underpinning a process, rather than an agenda to which people are invited consciously to subscribe. The really remarkable thing is that, for a period of time now beginning to approach a hundred years (though whether it will make it to the complete century is a more open question), the study of literary texts in the English language has received a kind of quasi-automatic acceptance as one of the given features of school life, and that this acceptance has come from teachers, parents, pupils and even employers. I call this acceptance remarkable because, on the face of it, studying literature does not greatly generate capacity, taking this either in a restricted sense to mean the equipping of pupils to go on to become professional writers, or, in a more extended meaning, understanding it as consisting of the fostering and development of non-literary communicative skills. It is only in very recent years, and in such developments as the relative marginalization of English literature within the structure of the GCSE examination process, that significant cracks in this broad consensus have begun to appear.

The early career of English as a school subject in its own right has been the subject of many studies, and I shall do no more here than touch on a number of themes more fully developed elsewhere. Part of the prestige of the subject derived from its role as a kind of *ersatz* classics. A good deal of the approval it received at various official levels came from its perceived utility as an inculcator of the kind of cultural nationalism I described in Chapter 1 – though it is as well to remember that it was only by degrees that it was differentiated from other vectors such as the study of English history in this respect. The framework of institutional provision of education established by the 1902 Education Act could be said to create both the need and the opportunity for this kind of subject provision within secondary education. The war of 1914–18 offered only too graphically the instance of a nearly successful enemy, relatively new as a unitary nation state, but capable of drawing on a heritage of high culture, composed over a much longer period, as one of its forms of ideological support. The revolutions and civil disturbances which occurred throughout Europe during the concluding years of the war and its immediate aftermath gave added urgency to the quest for educational material that could validate the assumptions of a shared heritage and a national unity that transcended the bounds of class or region.

Yet within this broad development various contradictions were present from the very beginning. The study of the classics was the province of the gentleman, but, demographically, the school study of English literature was from the beginning preponderantly the province of the middle classes, and the 1944 Education Act widened the social base further again. Whereas classics was very largely a male preserve, the development of English coincided with, and drew upon, the increasing numbers of women in the teaching profession, and when it has been an optional subject it has tended to attract significantly greater numbers of girls than of boys. The fact that access to the texts was not achieved via the study of the syntax and lexicon of a foreign language led to the assumption that it was an 'easy' subject – and this assumption interacted with other assumptions about the gender of its practitioners, to produce a negative, or at least ambiguous, image of the subject within a male-dominated culture.

Another set of contradictions, however, derived from the fact that the classics had been the product not just of different linguistic systems but of empires and societies very different from those of the young Englishmen, and women, now studying the subject. The essence of all that was best in these societies was held somehow to have been infused into each student generation: 'Conquered Greece conquered Rome', which in turn conquered, through being in some way the precursor of, the British Empire. Yet at the same time Latin was inescapably recognized to have been, through most of its existence of over two millennia as an available language system, the transnational, transcultural language for communication within Europe and even beyond. So classics, and particularly Latin, when seen as a proto-nationalism, was particularistic and characterized by affinity; when seen as a culturally neutral linguistic system, it was universalistic and characterized by a meritorious difficulty in acquisition.

The one opportunity for 'English' to achieve meritorious difficulty was for it to be held to be grounded in the study of Anglo-Saxon, but this option was decisively rejected within the schooling system, and became embedded only in the undergraduate courses in English offered by certain universities, Oxford being prominent amongst these. Henceforward, therefore, the only difficulties of this kind that the subject could offer were the relatively low-level ones of using a standard syntax and orthography. This is not to say, of course, that achieving these skills was either easy or universally accomplished, particularly in a language as class-inflected as English is; however, these inflections were not themselves capable of being developed into a sufficiently substantial formal classroom body of knowledge of a kind appropriate to the overt subject-matter of schooling, however much finely-nuanced discrimination and embarrassment they might give rise to in such a setting. In any event, to have formalized them in this way would have been to have pulled the rug from under the ideology of a common 'Englishness'.

But if 'English', taken as a language, was presented as a largely transparent medium of communication, then the ostensible object of study had to be the literary works that were recognized as canonical; furthermore, these were often presented as being generative of, rather than being generated by, the language medium itself. It is probable that this book will be read by at least one reader who can recall being told that Middle English was invented by Chaucer so that he could write *The Canterbury Tales*. It is curious to reflect that this notion of artists as linguistic innovators was being propounded at about the same time that the Russian Formalists were developing the same theme in very different circumstances; in the English version, however, the new language form is not unique to literariness, but instantly becomes the common language of the whole society.

In Chapter 2 I quoted the Newbolt Report's disparaging comments on much current English teaching as being 'conventional and divorced from reality'. Doyle (1989), commenting on the recurrent use of these and similarly evaluative expressions within the Report, refers to its 'particular appropriations of the deceptively simple terms "experience" and "life"' (p. 45). He then continues:

This is achieved by treating highly selective versions of experience as if they covered the whole range of experiential processes and forms of living, which, in fact, excludes the normal experiences and lives of the vast majority of the population. The same applies to the Committee's use of the term 'reality' which, when placed in significant opposition to 'convention', refers back to the same selective cultural parameters. The point of this exercise is to limit the terms experience, life, and reality in such a manner as to enable the claim that popular access to all three can only be gained by means of art which, for the purposes of national education, effectively means English and especially English Literature.

What all this amounted to was an implied parallel between 'experience' and 'life' on the one hand, and the successful use of standard English and its associated orthography on the other: the appropriation of terms that appeared to relate to the whole population, its experiences and its skills, but in practice were clearly seen as the province of one particular segment of the nation – its culture, its manner of speech, and the extension of the latter into the written medium of communication.

This notion that the Newbolt Report articulated – that art expresses a higher reality than day-to-day living, especially that experienced by the great bulk of the population, can provide – is of course another assumption that can be traced back to neo-platonic versions of the role of the classics in the educational process. For such a notion to be effective, the texts themselves had to be seen as in some way transcending their circumstances of origin, and constituting a harmonious whole. This harmonious wholeness in some way preceded, and also transcended, the linguistic medium through which it was expressed, rather than being a product of the medium. For this reason it was an act bordering on the redundant, perhaps even a solecism, to examine the 'conventions' that, from an altogether different viewpoint, might be held to be constitutive of the text. By this means, then, both rhetoric and sociology were removed as possible means to an understanding of the works in question, and history was differentiated into a separate discipline. By the same stroke, the teachers of English had their professional status established and assured; henceforward they could claim to be the gatekeepers who permitted access to 'life', this access, of course, only being attainable via the approved access to approved works.

As regards the English texts themselves, it proved relatively easy to ignore the fact that Elizabethan and Jacobean drama, and also to a certain extent the eighteenth century novel, were in origin by no means the products of high culture, since they could be held to have transcended their original nexus in becoming part of the national heritage. Nevertheless, the subject matter of a great number of novels, from the 1840s onwards, was quite explicitly the threat, encapsulated in the phrase 'The Two Nations', to an assumed national unity. Even less easy to ignore was the fact that so many highly-esteemed novels of the late eighteenth and the nineteenth century were written by women, and to a considerable degree for women. It is my supposition that it was partly to overcome this apparent difficulty that the proponents of cultural nationalism laid so much stress upon the lyric poem (and, by backward extension, upon the 'lyric' qualities of dramatists such as Shakespeare) since the authors in question were almost exclusively male, and maleness was deeply implicit in the whole notion of cultural nationalism, just as it was explicit in the ideological maintenance of empire.

Lyrical poetry has further advantages over the novel, where harmoniousness is concerned: it relates to the mood of the moment, depicts the experiences of an individual rather than a group, is often elegiac, and operates more readily in an arcadian than an industrial setting. In addition, of course, its typically short length makes it a more convenient vehicle for classroom practices ranging from memorization through admiration to particular types of self-authenticating discussion. In fact, these perceived virtues of brevity, elegiac nostalgia, and concentration on the individual sensibility were so attractive that they were on occasion extended to works of prose fiction, with titles such as *The Boyhood of David Copperfield* being created by one bold stroke of an editor's pen, the text in question being removed like a rib from the side of a sleeping Charles Dickens.

A significant difference between the corpus of English literature and that of the classics, however, was in the absence from the former, at least for the purposes of educational processes, of a major national verse epic. If only there had been available some equivalent to *The Aeneid*, one is tempted to conclude, how much easier life would have been for the compilers of syllabuses. However, putting the issue in this way immediately highlights the difference between the role of the epic in a classical education and any function it might have had in an English-based one. The unfolding plot structure of *The Aeneid* is deliberately and self-consciously a work of empire, as the scion of a royal house re-establishes its fortunes elsewhere under the seal of divine approval. As an exemplar of filial piety and territorial acquisitiveness, Aeneas might well offer a role model for the future rulers over palm and pine. However, the monolithic 'nobility' which is the feature of the epic sits less happily, for reasons discussed elsewhere in this chapter, in a system designed for the education of much larger segments of the population.

This 'nobility' in the context of an epic poem in English was most to be found in the work of Milton, and the history of its reception, especially in the context of schooling, merits more detailed treatment than it will receive here. Amongst literary critics, *Paradise Lost* has been exposed to the uneasy and distant respect of Johnson, to the demonologizing of Eliot, and to a variety of uncomfortable responses in between. It was Johnson who first pointed out that the poem is unique amongst epics in not providing a human figure with whom a readership might identify; he was also more honest than Eliot in recording the importance of Milton's typification as a regicide. If we add this to Blake's more incisive comment that Milton was on the Devil's side without knowing it, we can begin to identify some of the ambiguities that made the work far too double-edged for the purposes of an educational system and an educational canon.

But, though the national epic did not exist in the form that would have been so convenient to the compilers of syllabuses, a version of the epic was every-where available – the comic epic in prose that was Fielding's definition of the novel. I suggested earlier that novels characteristically gave more difficulty to the compilers of syllabuses than did lyric poetry. It is as well to be quite practical about this: anyone who has ever worked in a classroom is well aware of the problems of 'teaching' in one term what was originally written as a three-decker. But there are difficulties of other kinds as well. Anyone teaching *The Aeneid* has the methodological advantage (if that is what it is) of dealing with a genre that nowadays exists only within the covers of the set book. By contrast, the novel was a predominant form of entertainment until the development of electronic media during this century, and is still sufficiently attractive to a sufficiently large audience to make large incomes available to successful authors, and to place their works from time to time upon supermarket shelves. A genre which is so pervas-ive is one which is intrinsically difficult to define at all exclusively in terms of the 'high' purposes of cultural nationalism, and it is worth considering that most instances of conflict between parents and teachers over the perceived suitability of classroom material still seem to revolve around novels rather than anything else.

In part such difficulties can be addressed by the construction of a canon – by defining some works as intrinsically good and others as beyond the pale and doubtless written only for the low purposes of giving pleasure and generating wealth. The concept of a canon, and its effective policing, are more important than the substantive content of the canon at any one time; definitions have famously shifted within universities, within schools, and in the uneasy space that lies between them. But I suspect that the difficulties that novels pose in respect to the construction of a cultural-nationalist syllabus are more radical than this. They relate to the definition of what a novel is and how it talks.

Standard histories of literature trace the point of origin of the novel to differ-ent dates in different cultures: to Pushkin, less than two hundred years ago, in Russia; to a date perhaps a century earlier in England. But then such accounts become entangled in essentialist definitions: does the prose writing of the Res-toration, or of Elizabethan England, count or not? If the answer to such questions is yes, what is there then that legitimately disqualifies Malory's *Morte d'Arthur* from being considered a novel? What of the Greek romances that Bakhtin discussed?

However, a novel can be defined in other and perhaps more important ways than those of immutable essences, or indeed of simple chronology; as a literary genre, it was not something which just appeared like a rabbit out of a magician's hat, and, as my reference to Malory suggests, it may be helpful in any case to try to provide a definition which distinguishes between different processes which may be exemplified by different genres, but are not necessarily confined to them. Bakhtin attempted to do something of the kind when he differentiated what he called the polyphony of the novel from the homophony or single-voicedness of the epic. One way of attempting to explain what he intended to convey through these terms is that a powerful narrating voice and teleological intention steers us through *The Aeneid*, within which Aeneas has no independent voice or existence, whereas in *The Brothers Karamazov* it sometimes seems as though the characters may be about to take over, like (in the later phrase) lunatics in charge of the asylum, and steer both dialogue and narrative towards goals of their own. This is polyphony of an extreme kind, and it is interesting to note the resemblance between Bakhtin's definition here and that of more conservative accounts of the novel and its dialogue, in which the pleasant hum of conversation replicates that of life, and the existence of 'rounded', larger-than-life, and somehow free-standing characters validates, and is validated by, their taken-for-granted existence in the world beyond the novel. But in Bakhtin, for at least some of the time, it meant a lot more than this.

Pechey (1989:45) has pointed out that, whereas for Bakhtin in the 1920s polyphony amounted to truth and homophony to error, some ten years later he had come to achieve a more political vision in which he saw each of these types of utterance as the outcome of different social processes. It is thus no longer a matter of saying that the novel is 'true' (for which read true-to-life, resembling real spoken dialogue, showing and approving a society in which diversity is valued) and the epic the opposite (tendentious, author-driven, ideologically-motivated) since that implies that these two modes can be judged from some pre-existent ground, untainted by language or rhetoric, on which such sweeping statements can be promulgated. Rather it becomes a matter of finding out what such uses of language do to the people who receive them, and perhaps are intended to do. It transfers questions about the uses of language from the realms of philosophy and linguistics to those of social science and politics.

Reverting then to the question of what a novel is and how it can be distinguished from other forms of prose (or indeed verse) writing, it is, I want to suggest, helpful to look at the kinds of definition that Bakhtin offered. The first requirement that he proposed is a historical and linguistic one, namely that the various vernaculars should become, as they did at the time of the Renaissance, the accepted media for published writing. This then produces a situation in which they are both various between themselves (as opposed to the uniformity of Latin) and standard within the social and material spheres in which they are deployed.

The second requirement, however, is both social and political on the one hand, and stylistic on the other, since it is concerned with the deployment of a range of 'voices' within the text of the novel corresponding to the diversity of forms of speech to be encountered within society. This heteroglossia (or range of varieties of speech) then becomes the characteristic and defining feature of the language in which novels are written, but it can only be produced, or even envisaged, by writers who, like Dostoyevsky, live in a world which has experienced the social and physical upheavals of urbanization and industrialization, and has seen the confrontation and interaction, at a micro-level of social activity, that takes place between people with different class affiliations and class interests.

Once these conditions have been met, it is not, however, necessary to assume that the individual writers of individual novels are in some way making a radical or even political statement, at least of a progressive nature, in producing the texts that they do; indeed, in the case of authors such as Dostoyevsky or Balzac, it would be very difficult indeed to justify such statements. Rather, it is the case that the language – or the languages – available to them to write novels in take care of that by themselves.

This heteroglottic language is, in its modern realization, a feature of the novel, but in Bakhtin's depiction of things it has a longer history than this. In its capacity to subvert, parody, and undermine the voice of authority generally, it is a functional equivalent of the medieval carnival, in which the combined speech and actions of the participants did very much the same sort of thing. Heteroglottic language is therefore both modern in that it derives from certain achieved social processes and changes, and also traditional in that it expresses a continuity with medieval disruptiveness and licensed opposition to authority.

It is always interesting to notice the way in which the combination of tradition and innovation to be found in the various devices and structures within the novel is dealt with by the various theorists and critics who have to come to terms with it. Famously, or notoriously, the Marxist theoretician Lukács did so by extolling the bourgeois novel of the nineteenth century for the openness of its depiction, through the device of realism, of a social transformation in a way that somehow overrode the conscious intentions of its often reactionary authors. In contrast, he pilloried modernist texts of the twentieth century for wilful subjectivism and mystification, regardless of the frequently more impressive political credentials of those who had written them.

In British writing, the cultural pessimism of F. R. Leavis, antithetically opposed in many ways to the obligatory optimism of Lukács, made a partial exception for certain canonical texts of the present century. Having done so, he then traced a continuity from them, reaching back through their nineteenth-century realist predecessors (such as Lukács had praised) to an idealized past in which a community of spirit produced a community of language. In this way, the parallels and lines of development that he draws, and the approval that he confers, are distinctly similar to Bakhtin's, even though, in Bakhtin's terminology, it is a monoglossia rather than a heteroglossia that, Leavis would maintain, provides the continuity.

Two other curious points of similarity between Bakhtin and Leavis are worth noting in this connection. The first concerns the relative marginalization of the author in respect of his finished text. 'Never trust the artist; trust the tale' was the citation from D. H. Lawrence that Leavis frequently used. Bakhtin's position varied more than somewhat between one publication and the next, but it is significant that, in his revision of his book on Dostoyevsky, he took particular care to emphasize that the author was no more than the culmination of a long process of popular narration, and indeed in certain important ways no more than the current outcome of it.

The second point of similarity concerns the role allotted to an agrarian society in the schematization that each provided. Despite what I have said earlier about the importance of urbanization and industrialization in the generation of new types of dialogue between individuals, it was to the carnival crowd in the town square of a pre-industrial society that Bakhtin turned for an illustration of a language that was securely grounded in bodily knowledge and not susceptible to the wiles of an official ideology. Leavis's devotion to the virtues of pre-industrial life and language are too well-known to require illustration.

It is important, however, not to overstate the similarities between Bakhtin and Leavis, especially as some of them may prove more apparent than real in any event. One major point of difference between them requires, moreover, to be mentioned at this point. The thrust of Leavis's work was towards the creation of a canon, which was oppositional in respect of certain features of the 'official' canon of his day, but which aspired in the end to fulfil largely similar functions in respect of a clearly-defined national culture. In contrast, Bakhtin, though he had his heroes such as Dostoyevsky and Rabelais to whom he returned again and again, was in profound opposition to the whole notion of a canon, considering it an aspect of an official and imposed culture, against which was pitted the derisive mockery of carnivalesque language. So, whilst Leavis identified with the defenders of the citadel, Bakhtin's sympathies were with the leaderless and polyglot crowd surrounding it.

An equally important difference is to be found between the terms of fact and value that Lukács and Bakhtin used in their accounts of the nineteenth-century realist novel. In comparing it to the epic, Lukács was bestowing on it the highest praise available to him; it captured and represented a movement in history, following it through from A to Z, and treating its characters as representative and enactive of this process. But while Lukács valued progression, Bakhtin was all for interruption, disruption, and dispersal; against the tyranny of the forward impulsion of the narrative, he preferred the multifarious and disorganized variety of dialogue, with all the threat that this offers to linear narrative movement. This is a point that can be made in other ways, through other systems and other metaphors. Barthes might have described it, using the terms of his theory of narratology, as a liking for indices rather than nuclei; Jakobson, in another use of structuralist contrasts, as a preference for the paradigmatic rather than the syntagmatic. At all events, whereas Lukács saw in his favoured novelists of the nineteenth century the triumphant continuation of all that was valuable in the epic, Bakhtin would want to assert that they provided the *coup de grâce*.

What all this means, for the construction of the literature elements of a school curriculum, is that decisions have to be made which may have a bearing on the development and maintenance of an educational canon, but which are also more radical and far-reaching. In the course of this process, the attention that is given to novels is central, both because they are themselves possible sources for a major part of the printed matter that pupils may be required to read, and also because the kind of attention that is given to them by the educational process, the kinds of understandings that pupils may take from them, and the kinds of teaching activity that may be constructed around them are in many ways exemplary for the educational process as a whole.

I pointed out earlier that the effective absence of Anglo-Saxon from any part of the school curriculum represented a 'lost opportunity' as far as the notion of meritorious difficulty was concerned. Its felt absence has, however, been a kind of hidden undercurrent in various forms of cultural and educational discourse from time to time. In a weaker parallel to forms of German Romanticism, and indeed to notions of ethnic purity that can be found uncomfortably nearer to home, it has sometimes been claimed to represent a 'pure' form of English, in contrast to the 'adulteration' it received with the infusion of Norman French, and indeed the speech of sundry other, and subsequent, lesser breeds without the law. But this approach has never represented a consistently significant attitude to matters of political ethnolinguistics, since it has had to compete, in the minds of those most likely to be receptive to it, with the English version of the notion of the 'melting pot' – to quote Kipling again, the assertion that 'Saxon and Norman and Dane are we'.

Crowley (1989) draws attention to an interesting discrepancy, as he sees it, in Bakhtin's thinking on the subject of the development of standard languages. It was Bakhtin's claim that the establishment of proto-national vernaculars (French, Italian, etc.) at the time of the Renaissance was a move from monoglot Latin (monoglot, that is, in terms of the chosen vehicle for the discourse of power) towards polyglot variety. Yet clearly, as far as the exercise of power within the nascent or developing nation states was concerned, the national language had a strongly monoglottic function.

It is Crowley's contention that the anti-authoritarian streak in Bakhtin causes him to overstate, or at least to over-generalize, the virtues of heteroglossia within the context of political action and political consciousness. Crowley himself sees the increasing use of a standard in the nineteenth and twentieth centuries as very much a two-edged weapon. On the one hand it is clearly facilitative for the development of imperial power, both as regards those who are to be ruled by the imperium, and as regards those who are to be recruited to minor and subsidiary roles within the structure of empire. On the other hand it provides those who are subordinated to power with the means to organize against it.

Crowley takes care to emphasize here that the progressive aspects of monoglossia are specific to particular times and places. In post-revolutionary America, or in the Italy of the late nineteenth and early twentieth centuries, the availability of a common language was instrumental in the co-ordinated opposition to external rule. However, in other colonial situations – Crowley offers the example of the Ireland of James Joyce, and his account in *A Portrait of the Artist as a Young Man* of Stephen's feelings of inadequacy of language when talking to the Dean – the use of the standard language is alienating and disabling.

It would be interesting and informative to consider this argument in a wide variety of contexts. Here, I shall offer just two. One concerns the possible utility of English as a unifying language for the co-ordination of opposition to British rule in India, as opposed to the use of any one Indian language for the same purpose. In such an extravagantly heteroglottic a place as India, it is at least arguable that the advantages of a standard language that was (geographically) widely available and that, unlike Hindi, did not favour one part of the country, might have outweighed its connotations as the language of the ruler. However, the history of its use by Indians both before and after independence suggests that other factors weighed equally strongly.

The second instance is that of the co-ordination of working-class protest movements across Britain from the end of the eighteenth century to the last of the great Chartist movements. It has been pointed out that what was alleged to be a restricted code of speech was clearly no impediment to the conception and implementation of an integrated mass movement. By the same token, the fact that most local planning, and much national co-ordination, was carried out in a variety of regional dialects seems to have been neither a practical nor a symbolic impediment.

I imagine that Crowley and I might therefore agree that neither monoglossia nor polyglossia is automatically a sign of political virtue or a guarantee of political effectiveness, just as earlier in this chapter I pointed out that a truth value cannot be ascribed either to polyphony or to homophony. Rather, each must be considered in its context of operation in order to try to determine what particular consequences will ensue from its use.

In the context of education, then, I think it is possible to suggest that there is likely to be one great advantage to be derived from exposure to the heteroglottic aspects of the novel form. Just as 'English' is a construct produced by selection and exclusion from the various languages and dialects that have been, and are today, used in these islands, and the great range of written and oral forms that have been pressed into service to assist the ends of these varous users, so the novel is 'un-English' in the way in which it can remind us of diversity by forcibly presenting us with the inscribed evidence of difference.

What it is open to the English teacher to do, then, is to work towards two quite separate goals, which it is important to distinguish. The means to accomplish this end is to enable a class to differentiate between, again in Bakhtin's terms, interpretation and criticism, the first being grounded in belief, the second in scepticism. In the first of these activities, the reader is engaged in conversation with the writer, reaching out towards a long-distance partner in a social dialogue. In the second, the reader is functioning as a social scientist, arranging, ordering, and comparing the signs of the text. In a late essay, entitled 'The Problem of the Text' (1986), Bakhtin describes these activities in terms which for once approach those of Foucault when discussing archaeological practices – though of course Foucault would have been much more chary of accepting the concept of the absent partner in Bakhtin's view of interpretation.

In the second of these two modes, that of the sceptical and critical analyst, Bakhtin pictures a kind of steady regression from the immediacy of the work-as-utterance through the various languages of which it is an example. It is to a greater or lesser degree characteristic of the language of the author; it is characteristic of a particular genre (an issue I discuss further in Chapter 9); it is written in a particular language; it demonstrates the possibilities of language as a system.

In the light of the points made a few paragraphs back, I would myself prefer not to see this as a picture with a single perspective, but, so to speak, as one with different vanishing points, since more than one language, or genre, or dialect, or type of authorial inflection can be found within one particular work, so that it is at the point of intersection of multiple vistas. But what I do find particularly valuable in Bakhtin's work at this point is his bracketing together of the actions of the everyday reader and those of the research scholar in his definition of the 'reactive text' that they both produce. Using the analogy of the research physicist, whose observations at a sub-atomic level are influenced by the fact that an observer is there as part of the process, he depicts the social scientist as someone whose responses to the material under investigation are part of the data to be investigated.

Extending the concept of the scholar to include the pupil, it then becomes possible to see how both the observable features of the text, in all its variousness, and the classroom responses to it, in all their variety, can with some justification be described as the subject matter of the English curriculum. The responses, however, would then include not only the interpretive and affective aspects which the teachers quoted in Chapter 2 would appear to be angling for, but also the more language-oriented types of categorization and analysis which what we could call 'classroom scholarship' might produce. This analytical, sceptical type of analysis, taken as a counterweight to the pedagogical commitment to personal growth, would enable teachers and pupils to investigate not only what English *is*, but also what it is *for*.

6 Diagnoses and prescriptions

Of the 557 pages that comprise the main text of the Bullock Report, only 15 are explicitly devoted to the role of literature and its place in schooling. In retrospect this small proportion can seem slightly surprising, since, in the collective professional memory at least, Bullock stands at the apogee of the integration of literature into the wider processes and practices of English teaching, as well as of the movement to diffuse the insights of this particular subject on a cross-curricular basis.

In other respects, though, it is not surprising at all. This is particularly so if we remind ourselves of what was at the time the popular expectation of what the Report was to do. Despite the inclusiveness of the title of the published report (*A Language for Life*), the Bullock Committee's remit was, during the period in which it was being written, generally perceived to be quite a narrow one, concentrating on the alleged decline in reading standards, and on possible ways of remedying the situation. So much was this the case that the authors of the Introduction to the Report felt obliged to stress that their terms of reference were wider than this interpretation supposed, covering 'all aspects of teaching the use of English, including reading, writing, and speech' and that they interpreted their brief 'as language in education, and have ranged from the growth of language and reading ability in young children to the teaching of English in the secondary school' (p. xxxi). This seemed at the time, and still seems, a successful bid to humanize and professionalize what might originally have been a narrow and technicist process of investigation, even if the effort of achieving it shows from time to time, not only in the clear tensions that exist between one chapter and another, but also sometimes inscribed within the text of individual sections.

To indicate one form that this humanization takes, the two quotations with which the Report opens its discussion of literature teaching (from Nowell Smith in 1917 and the Newsom Report in 1963) have in common the use of the concept of 'civilizing' in relation to the effect of literature on school pupils. Subsequent discussion makes it clear that this does not represent a commitment on the part of the Report to the concept of cultural heritage – though some aspects of this model are possibly still vestigially present, as in the neutrally reported suggestion (p. 130) that some teachers, believers in the value of 'discernment', see literary classics as something with which pupils should be endowed. Though we are told that there is a 'polarity of view' on this particular question, disagreement within the profession in general is represented as largely absent, and where it is found it is discerned not in relation to the 'value' of literature in school, but in respect of the 'treatment' (p. 124) it receives there. Furthermore, this disagreement is found not within British staffrooms or professional associations, but, so to speak, in mid-Atlantic, with 'many' American teachers concentrating on studies of image and symbol in a way that we may conjecture derives from New Criticism (though the Report does not identify it as such), whereas 'In Britain the tradition of literature teaching is one which aims at personal and moral growth' (p. 125). Neither cultural heritage nor skills, then, were portrayed as major parts of what was then the current British professional agenda. Furthermore, although the Report finds many examples of unimaginative and stultifying classroom practices, its overall picture is unmistakably an optimistic one, describing a teaching force largely open to the prospect of collective professional development, and one in which a commitment to the personal growth of pupils clearly predominates. To a considerable degree this optimism must have been generated by the systematic and frequent visits to schools that were undertaken, even if to some extent it also emanated from the convictions and enthusiasm of the authors.

The commitment to the 'personal growth' approach to literature is not just assumed, but is argued for. Two familiar contentions are advanced in its favour. The first is that literature offers an extension of pupils' vicarious experience and an invitation to empathize with the very different lives of those they read about. The second, an inversion though not a contradiction of the first, is that pupils can 'at the safety of one remove' read a depiction of features that characterize their own lives also. But I have perhaps put this last point more generally than the Report chooses to do, since in describing the state of pupil/readers it speaks specifically of their 'personal difficulties and . . . feelings of deficiency' (p. 125). So, although the personal growth approach in general tends towards a Rousseauesque belief in the validity of children's conceptual systems at any given point in time, there is here at least the ghost of a deficit model more readily associable with the cultural heritage model.

There then follows an argument which I find very difficult to untangle. 'The media' (clearly used as a pejorative term here in the spirit of *Mass Civilization and Minority Culture*) are criticized for presenting euphoria as the natural state of life, so it may be inferred that the presentation of 'difficulties' is an appropriate counterweight, offered by a richer cultural tradition. Studies of children's unguided reading preferences are then cited as an indication of the value of the activity of reading as a personal resource. Children, we are told, derive enjoyment in this way, and also compensation for the difficulties of growing up. But though, from decade to decade, the list of the most popular books is composed of different and changing items, the features that the items have in common across the years are wish fulfilment, lack of subtlety, and formulaic plotting with an invariable happy ending. In contrast to all this, the kind of literature to which teachers must try to introduce pupils consists of those books 'where a complexity of relationships enlarges . . . understanding of the range of human possibilities' (p. 126).

I take this paragraph to hover uneasily between two differing ideas: that all reading, no matter of what, is ultimately an expansion of vicarious emotional experience and therefore a good thing, and the alternative view that it is only exposure to good, demanding, complex and difficult literature that actively promotes personal growth. This latter view receives some corroboration in the comments on fantasy literature, which I discuss below.

Continuing to draw on survey work, the Report then discusses the declining incidence of voluntary reading during the early teenage years, and the role that the teacher can undertake in compensating for this by continuing to maintain a record of pupils' reading once they have passed on from the stage at which they are dependent upon reading schemes. To be able to be effective in this area, teachers must maintain their knowledge, perhaps on a pooled basis, of what is available in the way of fiction, especially good modern children's literature, to which the Report is particularly wedded. The concluding paragraphs of the chapter, incidentally, make a similar point with regard to preparation for the teaching of poetry. By means of a good overall professional knowledge of available fiction, teachers can compensate for what is seen as a preponderance of non-fiction titles in schools' stockholdings, and supplement such activities as history projects by introducing novels that offer differing and mutually contrasting perspectives on the topic matter. They can also make suggestions for further reading that appropriately match the pupil's own individually expressed interests.

At the same time, the Report is suspicious of the denaturing of fiction that occurs when original works are filleted for passages that are relevant to thematic work, or when pupils' experience of literature is derived entirely from anthologized passages. The danger that it perceives in thematic study is that it ignores the complexity of the work from which the passage derives. Though the educational value of shared talk and discussion on the given theme is considerable, and though this approach avoids the 'dryness of schematic analysis' (p. 132) it can mean that the extract itself is treated merely as a springboard rather than as an object of study in its own right. Anthologies should therefore consist of complete pieces, or at least long extracts, which can be given appropriate attention as 'virtually artistic units on their own'. It should be emphasized here that the interest in 'artistic units', at least at an overt level, is not to do with some variety of aesthetic contemplation, but relates to the opportunities afforded to pupils to engage in close reading along the whole curve of the development of a narrative. The issue, in short, relates to one particular type of reading competence.

One type of activity, and one type of book, are particularly commended. Small group discussion between pupils who have recently read a particular book is to be preferred to other forms of follow-up activity, especially 'the obligatory written book review' (p. 128). Books written in the narrative mode figure so largely in the tables of those chosen and read for pleasure that they should form an appropriately large part of a school's stockholding of books designed to be individually selected and read. The attractiveness of narrative is, in general, reported rather than analysed. One category of narrative is, however, singled out for particular attention. Fantasy, fairy-tale, and folk-tale are esteemed for their (unspecified) 'deep significance' and for being a counterweight to 'a circumscribed domestic situation with narrow limits of action and feeling' (p. 129). This, it appears, is particularly a problem for the working-class child, who can find little in early reading texts to which to relate. In devising a reading programme for this child, however, it is a misplaced kindness to concentrate on 'relevance' by excluding representations of everything except the familiar, since 'true relevance lies in the way a piece of fiction engages with the reader's emotional concerns' (p. 129).

There is a certain incoherence in the middle of the paragraph from which I have just quoted, which leads me to suspect that, despite the considerable length of the Report overall, there has been some editorial compression at this point. The discussion of the alienation of the working-class child, and the alleged need for relevant writing to address this problem, would suggest that the problem with too much reading matter was that it depicted an exclusively middle-class ambience. The preferred logic of combining depictions of the familiar and the unfamiliar, advocated earlier, would then suggest that a hefty dose of working-class realism was precisely what was required – for the sake of both middle- and working-class children. But, it seems, fantasy literature is being commended for its socially transcendent effects. Even if we grant the validity of this approach, it still seems odd that it is only the working-class children who are to do without the encouragement of encountering the familiar in literature.

Responsiveness and pleasure are important factors in the process of self-motivation – 'Learning how to appreciate with enthusiasm is more important than learning how to reject' (p. 132). The former is more valued by the authors of the Report than are the practices of close textual examination and summary, coupled with rote learning of trivial factual detail, as a preparation for examinations. These practices have expanded to such a degree that 'the literature has receded' (p. 130). Yet the authors recognize that teachers have difficulties in working with novels when their pupils have not grasped narrative sequences, and acknowledge that more work needs to be done on appropriate teaching strategies for such cases. They particularly applaud the effects of the newly-introduced CSE examination in encouraging extensive reading. In a significant minority of cases where inspired teaching takes place on O level courses, too, they find that pupils are not alienated by the subject.

The reference to narrative sequences quoted above could be taken to imply that a structured exposure to works of fiction of increasing narratological complexity should be an important aspect of the literature curriculum. The Report's preferred solution is a different one, and grounded upon an implicit agnosticism with regard to the possibility of classifying texts in order of difficulty, as would then be necessary. Since some titles were found to be set for the upper secondary years in one school, and the lower years in another, the possibility of a common professional agreement upon the levels of difficulty to be encountered in a given novel seemed remote. It seemed better, therefore, to adopt a saturation approach of encouraging wide individual reading.

This saturation approach returns us to the problem I signalled earlier in my discussion of the Report. It is, I think, defensible to adopt a position of believing that as wide and as varied as possible an exposure to fiction will contribute to an understanding of narrative devices, to intellectual growth and emotional development. It is also possible to adopt another position, which Bullock might have found too much akin to the American one, in which a structured exposure to narrative devices of gradually increasing complexity forms at least one organizing principle of the literature curriculum. Bullock appears to marshal a body of evidence for the latter argument, but to be deeply committed to the former one.

The Bullock Report was published in 1975. The Kingman Report appeared in 1988, and is the outcome of altogether different pressures and different defensive strategies, even if a number of its themes are still recognizable. In its opening pages it explicitly traces its own prehistory to James Callaghan's Ruskin College speech of 1976, as well as to Sir Keith Joseph's 1984 White Paper, and it speaks (p. 2) of the need for the rising generation to be adequately equipped not only to meet the demands of contemporary society (a goal that Bullock would have found by no means uncongenial) but also those of the competitive economy. Its chosen examples of the need for language competence relate to mortgage agreements, insurance claims, and washing-machine manuals – the world of individualism, capitalism, and consumerism. This notion of the use of English distances it in many ways from its predecessor – and yet there are many close links between the two reports, both acknowledged and unacknowledged. Kingman speaks of Bullock having had great influence on English teaching, and regrets that more of its recommendations have not been implemented (p. 2). A sentence such as 'The child should never be limited to reading or hearing only that which is embedded in everyday experience' (p. 8) could almost be a direct quotation from the kind of passage I discussed earlier. But it is the indirect quotations, and their new inflections, which are more telling.

In Bullock we can read 'fantasy, fairy-tale and folk-tale should take their place in the repertoire in the earliest stages of reading. J. R. R. Tolkien pointed out that fairy-tales were not evolved for the nursery; they found their way there by historical accident' (p. 129). The argument then proceeds to consider the affective and cognitive impact of such tales. When Kingman speaks of Tolkien and fairy-tales, however, it is to say 'Children who read Tolkien and then write their own fairy stories are engaged in a total process of language development which, among other advantages, may one day contribute to the writing of clear, persuasive reports about commerce or science' (p. 11). There is no echo here of Bullock's worry about 'narrow limits of action and feeling'. The earlier report, moreover, is concerned with the universal processes underlying the emotional development of the individual; the later one, though professedly written 'against the utilitarians', is making almost comically strenuous efforts to suggest that this process can have an economic payoff.

Like Bullock, Kingman is not centrally concerned with the place of literature in the English curriculum, and its greater brevity overall (it runs to a mere 71 pages of main text) would in any case inhibit any major contribution on this theme. Just as it disclaimed any intention to 'revisit the territory traversed so thoroughly by the Bullock Committee' (p. 3), so it referred onwards to the subsequent working group on English questions relating to 'the whole field of English, including literature and drama'. All this indicates that it would deliberately treat the topic of literature in a very elliptical fashion. But, though elliptical, it is knowing.

It takes care to point out on its first page that its membership includes those involved in 'academic language and literature studies', and eleven pages later it contrives to introduce a paragraph on the structuralist and post-structuralist revolutions in literary theory that is somewhat insecurely knitted into the surrounding text. The uses to which it puts these references are interesting. The paragraph preceding that dealing with literary theory had criticized the widespread school practice, during the 1960s and 1970s, of treating English lessons as 'no more than the setting for vigorous moral and social discussion, which too often assumed that language was a clear window onto a social world' (p. 12). Attention to the substance of language, and to literary genres, was therefore often perfunctory during these lessons. As we have seen, this is a criticism that could have been lifted directly from the pages of Bullock – though the interest in genre is perhaps a new concern. Recent theory, however, (and Saussure and Derrida are cited specifically here) centres on 'the relationship between the structures of language and the structures of our culture', and has made its influence felt in many different disciplines.

This is true, but it is hardly the whole truth. The influence of Saussurean thinking was after all hardly new, and neither was the subsidiary tradition of seeing language as the determinant of consciousness. Derrida's radical undercutting of the notion of a stable meaning is not only something that sets up challenges of various kinds to the Saussurean concept of *langue*, but is also at odds with most uses of the notion of tradition, and, as we shall shortly see, Kingman sets some store by one version of this notion.

For one of the things that Kingman contrives to do is to reinsert a number of telling and carefully-angled references to the whole notion of cultural heritage. This is done in a number of ways which it is tempting to label confused, but which, like the doubtfully successful attempt to yoke fantasy literature to commercial skills which I cited earlier, are possibly intended as a mixture of sops to Cerberus and more heartfelt, if more covert, statements of belief. Thus a paragraph which begins in Jakobsonian fashion by discussing the 'Aesthetic properties of language' (p. 11) proceeds to an unacknowledged paraphrase of Bullock concerning the need for the teacher to match the book to the pupil, and to introduce good contemporary works. But then it claims that it is equally important for the pupil 'to read and hear and speak the great literature of the past' (p. 11). What one expects to follow this is a claim that this non-contemporary literature is a source of continuing value in its own right. Instead, the Report talks of the persistent influence that classic works have on the rhythms of present-day speech and writing; thus the free verse of D. H. Lawrence (a 'modern' for the purpose of this exposition) echoes the rhythms of the Book of Common Prayer. The other two examples given are slightly more curious: *The Diary of Adrian Mole* apparently echoes the style of Dickens, and 'Hemingway's short sentences derive their power from their revolt against earlier, more discursive styles' (p. 11).

If an assertion such as this latter one is drawn from literary theory, it surely derives its parentage not from Saussure or Derrida, but from Harold Bloom. Acknowledging the past only to revolt against it – or revolting against it as a way of acknowledging it – is not only the way in which Bloom sees the Freudian relationship of a poet to his predecessors, but is also intrinsic to the way that this Report represents literature in use. Thus, as part of their reception of language, we are told that children amass a store of images, lines, phrases, rhythms, and ideas. This, we are given to understand, then allows greater possibilities for their production of language. Not only is this a skill that is of benefit to the individual; it is also the way to attend to 'the culture itself, which has to be revitalised by each generation' (p. 11). The words which I have just quoted are preceded by a genuflection to 'the powerful and splendid history of the best that has been thought and said in our language' which might have been drawn not from Bullock but from Newbolt. The sting in the tail, though, is that all this has to be 'revitalised', and, if pupils grasp what Hemingway is doing, revolted against as well.

There are then to be found in Kingman at least two levels of utterance on the subject of literature teaching. The exoteric one consists to obeisances to the proper quarters: Shakespeare, the Authorized Version, and a variety of other texts deemed, for the purposes of this exercise, perfectly non-controversial. A casual reading of the Report can then give grounds for assuming that all the proprieties have been observed, that tradition and continuing values are 'safe in our hands'. The esoteric one consists of a recognition that these Great Works are neither more nor less than *texts*, governed by conventions of genre, but pressing on and extending or even overturning the boundaries of these genres. Given such an understanding, there can then be seen to be a logical progression that leads from intertextuality to revisionism, or even to a deliberate flouting of a particular set of rules altogether. The Report quotes with obvious approval the comments of one of its witnesses concerning the opening of Dickens's *Bleak House* – a passage consisting of a string of verbless sentences. The particular interest of this passage concerned the effectiveness of the breach by skilled writers of normal rules of discourse 'as long as they know the rules in the first place' (p. 39). A further example of subversive intertextuality is then cited: Dickens's savagely indignant undeclared quotations from the Book of Common Prayer when describing the demeaning horrors of a pauper burial.

There then follows an extended comparison of various versions of the Anglican burial service from 1549 to 1970 (extraordinary, surely, in occupying at least one-fiftieth of the total text of the Report) coupled with a demonstration of how a study of orthography, rhythm, etymology, semantics, syntax, and discourse can illuminate the belief systems expressed by each version. Though it is nowhere expressly stated as such, this demonstration is meant to contrast with the reported practice in the 1960s and 1970s (p. 12) of proceeding straight to social comment and criticism without examining the linguistic texture.

If intertextuality leads to revisionism, precisely the same can be said of the connections between Kingman and Bullock. I have tried to draw attention to the curious relationship – well worthy in its own right of the attentions of Bloom – that exists between these two documents. The more recent one is studiously courteous to its predecessor, but one reads it, to begin with, expecting to find a sub-text that is contemptuous of such a manifestation of 1970s progressivism. What is actually there to be discovered is a more radical, if covertly expressed, view of the functioning of literature within schooling, in which the value of canonical works is not treated as static and given, and in which the mechanisms of change are located not within the individual consciousness but within the culture and the language.

It would doubtless have been fascinating to have been a fly on the wall when either the Bullock or the Kingman Report was being put together, and to see how the compromises necessary to produce a composite and agreed text were achieved. In the case of the National Curriculum proposals for English, it is possible to obtain an effect a little similar to this by comparing 'English for Ages 5 to 11', published in November 1988, with 'English for Ages 5 to 16', which appeared in June 1989.

The latter text incorporates a version of the former one. In some cases, words and paragraphs have been re-edited simply to accommodate a wider brief. In others, there is a conscious and avowed response to the reaction provoked by the first document. The most often noted instance of this is the list of authors provided by '5 to 11' for possible use in primary schools. This is absent in '5 to 16', which comments rather wearily (para. 1.21): 'Despite our firm statements to the effect that the list was purely illustrative and that there were no doubt omissions, media attention centred on this list to the detriment of the other, more important recommendations in the Report.'

In such a case there is an explicit response to a clearly articulated public view. It would be interesting to know, however, what pressures led to the alteration of the following words, which appeared in para. 3.9 of '5 to 11'. 'Language enters individual and social life at many points, but the public is often not sufficiently well-informed for enlightened discussion to take place'. In '5 to 16' para. 2.10 has substituted 'The resolution of difficult issues of language in an increasingly multi-cultural society requires informed citizens.'

It could be thought that a rather arrogant view of the great unwashed has been replaced by a turn of phrase that is more democratically diffident. But a concern for democracy is clearly articulated in '5 to 11', which, after discussing (para. 3.16) the need for children to understand codes and conventions if they are to respond to a multi-media environment which transmits a range of messages by different means, concludes 'All this is an important part of the democratic principles which should underlie the English curriculum, and to which the Kingman Report rightly draws attention'. A long quotation from Kingman is then introduced to underscore this point. Para. 2.17 of '5 to 16', though, omits this ringing assertion, so that the claim stands in Kingman's name only, and truncates the quotation as well, omitting the crisply declaratory 'People need expertise in language to be able to participate effectively in a democracy. There is no point in having access to information that you cannot understand.' All this serves (on the most charitable interpretation) to remove from the original text the notion that, though democracy is a good thing, not all the voters are yet properly prepared for it. In so doing, however, it also weakens the notion that a linguistic-cum-educational intervention is a political one as well, and this pattern of editorial watering-down is frequently though not always to be seen operating in the various small changes that are introduced.

The end of Chapter 3 of '5 to 11', for instance, lists the variety of possible approaches to English teaching that presently exist. After a one-sentence summary of 'personal growth' it comments 'This view goes naturally along with the view that children's own native languages or dialects should be respected by the school' (para. 3.20). In para. 2.21 of '5 to 16', this contention has silently disappeared. Since both versions profess a respect for native languages or dialects (though insisting on the central importance of acquiring mastery of Standard English during schooling) it is difficult to resist the thought that this original yoking together would be read as a declaration of policy that it was felt inopportune to supply.

Even minute changes to the original text must have some significance, since it was thought necessary to make them at all. Para. 3.10 of '5 to 11' states:

> The curriculum should also have in mind education in a European context, with reference both to the position of English as an international language, and also to increasing labour mobility, and therefore inter-cultural contact, within the European Community, especially after 1992.

'5 to 16' has chosen to omit the word 'therefore', and in so doing renders the relationship between labour mobility and inter-cultural contact coincidental rather than causal. The suggestion that cultural contact might have an economic determinant was perhaps seen as rash in the prevailing climate.

One other omission and alteration should be noted at this stage. I referred earlier to the listing of possible approaches to English teaching that is provided at the end of Chapter 3 of '5 to 11'. The list includes personal growth and cultural heritage, which we have met before, and also 'cross-curricular' which is, broadly speaking, a 'language across the curriculum' approach. However, the list also includes 'adult needs', which can be summarized as consisting of functional communicative skills needed in later life (especially, it seems, in the workplace) and 'cultural analysis', which provides the pupil with a critical understanding of the production and distribution of meanings and values. The document then concludes 'it is clear . . . that the "adult needs" and "cultural analysis" views are more relevant to the later years of compulsory schooling than to the primary years' (para. 3.26).

This is in itself a curious emphasis to provide: it is not clear, for instance, why 'cultural heritage' (at least in anything approaching a 'high cultural' sense) should not also be reserved for the later years of schooling if the other two categories are to be. '5 to 16' does not provide an extended rationale, however, and it retains unaltered the comment in respect of adult needs. It then adds 'some aspects of "cultural analysis" are also more relevant to older children' (para. 2.27). The reason given for this more qualified version of the assertion is that primary children can also be taught to understand how they are being influenced by the mass media.

Admirable as this aim is, it is not altogether clear to me how analytical, as opposed to merely perceptive, it is expected that primary school children should be in this regard. There is also, it seems to me, a paradox in that it is still claimed that the 'adult needs' approach finds its true place only in the senior years. If a range of communicative skills can only be inculcated at that particular stage of development, despite the fact that children appear to begin to develop a sociolinguistic repertoire virtually from the day they utter their first word, it seems strange that the analysis of modes of communication – surely a higher-order activity – can begin much earlier.

Both versions of the document concur in offering a view of the pupil's language repertoire, and of the place of literature within the development of that repertoire, that is broadly akin to that of the Kingman Report as expressed some months earlier. Thus Shakespeare, in keeping with what I have called the exoteric presentation of the curriculum, is accorded the privilege of a paragraph to himself and a guaranteed place in the syllabus in terms that can only gladden the heart of the Prince of Wales. Yet it is acknowledged, with a nod towards a more esoteric awareness, that he may not be the repository of eternal values and meanings, and that his work may be interesting and valuable in the classroom precisely because it enables a contest over ascribed meaning and value to take place.

Both versions also subscribe to a belief that, as we have seen, can be traced back at least as far as to Bullock: namely, that literature is of educational value because of its presentation and quasi-objectification of both the familiar and the unfamiliar. What is not to be found in Bullock in the same way is an attention to the possibilities of using non-Anglo–American literature in the classroom as an instance of this general principle. It is not that Bullock is in any way hostile to this, and indeed it can be seen as a natural and justified extrapolation from its views on language variation. Rather, it is that the incidence of pupils of a variety of ethnic and cultural backgrounds was not then seen as a factor in the equation in the same way. Since both Kingman and the National Curriculum document (in both versions) do recognize such a factor, it would not then be surprising if they should be prepared to devote some curriculum space to the provision of appropriate works of literature.

Thus '5 to 16', in a reworking of the same point as expressed in '5 to 11', links pupils' experience of a range of reading about others to that of discovering more about themselves (para. 7.3) in a way that is by now remarkably familiar to us. It then explicitly proceeds in the next paragraph to connect this objective to the goal of increasing pupils' awareness of the existence of social and cultural diversity. Reading should also contribute to the undermining of stereotypes, to the presentation of alternative points of view, and to an understanding of the processes that lead to the formation of a canon, and to the under-representation of authors using dialect or (in a careful phrase) 'from certain social groups'.

All this sounds like the beginnings of a radical approach to the teaching of literature, and indeed to a degree it is. However, it is only a beginning. Thus the under-represented groups listed above are not there because many of the pupils may correspond to and identify with them; rather, they fall under the heading of 'the unfamiliar' rather than 'the familiar'. In the same way, the following paragraph (7.5) advocates the use of works from India or the Caribbean. However, this is not because these books, or at least their settings, may be familiar to some pupils, but because pupils (which can mean only white pupils here) should be 'introduced to the ideas and feelings of cultures different from their own'. By these means they are to 'gain a better understanding of the cultural heritage of English literature itself'. The point is weakened still further, and the resonances of that 'cultural heritage' amplified, by the ensuing discussion (para. 7.6) of the importance of recognizing names and quotations from Aesop or the ancient classical stories. This is to be undertaken both to facilitate understanding of allusion and to introduce 'forms of discourse and ways of thinking which were powerful in the past, from which our own culture has developed'. The enduring power of this belief is something that I discuss elsewhere in this book.

So in the end, it seems, the canon is still canonical. To adapt Saussure's famous definition, '5 to 16' has got as far as seeing literature as a 'system of differences', but it still cannot cope with the rider – 'without positive terms'. So at one moment '5 to 16' seems happy to recognize that literary texts are devices for producing meaning (I would prefer 'meanings'), and can be studied in the same way that is commonly applied to non-literary texts in the course of media education (para. 7.23); 'who is communicating with whom and why' and so on are the questions to ask. At another moment, (para. 7.18) the document seems perfectly at ease with its terminology when prescribing for GCSE study works 'of sufficient substance and quality to merit serious consideration', even though this is a palpable reversion to the vocabulary of the most unreconstructed version of the cultural heritage approach.

However, the most simple-minded of all the approaches that we ourselves could apply to these documents would be to expect a series of recommendations without fissures or internal contradictions to issue from various groups working to secure what they could within the structure of the National Curriculum. Instead, we should be glad that so many opportunities still exist to raise so many questions, and that there is still some kind of warrant to apply a critical examination to texts of all kinds – including these.

7 Sociology and narratology

In the course of this chapter I want to re-examine the substance of what I have been looking at in earlier ones, but this time adopting a more explicitly sociological perspective to look at what I have treated elsewhere in the light of more purely pedagogical or discursive phenomena. I am doing so because, whereas other disciplines do indeed devote various kinds of attention to the inter-relationship of school and society, this is an explicit and central theme of the sociology of education. In particular, I want to look at certain aspects of the central sociological question of how inequality is sustained and reproduced within society at large by the specific agency of schooling, and (the other side of this particular coin) how it produces its effects upon particular individuals. Finally, I want to see to what degree all of this applies to English teaching in just the same way that it does to all other areas of the curriculum, or whether it has any particular features that require to be identified.

A professed commitment to equality has been a longstanding and significant element in the public discourse of many of those responsible for education, and an awareness of inequalities of various kinds has long been a conspicuous feature of school reform initiatives of various kinds, originating from various parts of the political spectrum. To take examples solely from the past fifty years or so, it provided a significant part of the justification for 'secondary education for all' as proposed by the 1944 Education Act, and again, a little later, for the movement towards the adoption of the provision of comprehensive schools, when the arbitrary and unequal effects of bipartite secondary education were more widely realized. The same basic principles have also been called into play to oppose various forms of streaming.

Each of these developments and initiatives may be described as being either largely consensual in nature or as having a broadly left-wing character. A not completely dissimilar rhetoric of equality, however, has also been a feature of the discussion and eventual adoption by a Conservative government, in the late eighties, of a national curriculum. It can of course be argued that this venture is the product of a kind of 'hidden consensus' in which the partial and qualified support of the official Opposition has been a necessary, or at least facilitative, part of the whole process. The same cannot, however, be said of proposals for voucher schemes, or for the various types of partial or total privatization of schooling, which are very much the property of the political right. These moves towards privatization are, however, once more advocated through the terms of a rhetoric which purports to address questions of equality, and emphasizes the equilibrating effects of a market economy upon the options available to the individual consumer of education, as market forces work to eliminate the worst schools from the field, leaving only the best. 'Levelling up rather than levelling down' is still a favoured slogan in such quarters; the point that interests me is that the notion of levelling is represented as attractive.

It is, however, possible to analyse these developments and proposals in a different fashion, and along a different axis. In the terms used by Lynch (1989), a concentration upon secondary education for all, or upon the introduction of a standardized national curriculum, amounts to a preoccupation with *provision*, whereas attention to questions of streaming, or matters relating to school choice or allocation, indicates a preoccupation with *consumption*. Very crudely, we might also compare the opposed terms provision/consumption with another contrast in which the terms are equality of opportunity/equality of achievement.

Lynch's work is grounded in a reappraisal of theories and investigations concerned with the existence and deployment of a hidden curriculum in schools. This hidden curriculum can be summarized as consisting of a set of practices which differentially inculcate skills and attitudes in pupils in such a way as to reproduce the social class divisions of society. This process of inculcation is frequently termed the distribution of cultural capital, and it is argued that those best equipped to receive it (typically, those of the most privileged social class origins) are the ones who, consciously or unconsciously, are being prepared for success in post-school life. It is Lynch's argument that 'Social inequalities are reproduced through schools because schools are universalistic in their *provision relations*, and particularistic in their *consumption relations*' (p. 27). What this means may be paraphrased as follows. If schools, for example, refused to accept pupils with a surname beginning with a letter from the second half of the alphabet, or taught only fair-haired pupils to read and write, then the overt absence of any rational and equitable basis for their actions would remove any apparent legitimacy not only from their procedures for admission or the teaching of literacy, but also from their other actions as well. To preserve the appearance of equity, therefore, schools must offer what is seen to be a set of basic educational opportunities in a way which is seen to be open to all. This is the universalistic provision that Lynch speaks of, and a widespread belief in its existence is necessary for the legitimacy of the schooling process as a whole.

However, the ways in which this provision is put to work vary a good deal, and Lynch, whose own research work was conducted in the Irish Republic, focuses particularly on the role of mediating groups, and to some degree also on the ways in which the pupils themselves generate a variety of cultures and practices which affect the uses to which educational provision is put. For the purposes of this chapter, however, I shall wish to lay greater emphasis on the second of these two factors.

One important mediator is the classroom teacher, a large part of whose job satisfaction derives from a sense of having successfully promoted the process of learning in the classroom. Most frequently, as Lynch and others remind us, this occurs when dealing with pupils with whom the teacher can identify – and a shared social class affiliation is one of the likeliest causes of such identification. It is inevitable, then, that differently perceived social class characteristics exhibited by pupils will generate different types of micro-sequences in lessons. It can also be argued, as Bourdieu (1977) has done, that the *habitus*, or complex of beliefs and behaviour patterns characteristic of each social class, that appertains to each particular pupil will produce different degrees of receptivity to the acquisition of cultural capital.

I referred above to the teacher's experiences of satisfaction and reward when communicating effectively with pupils. But it is not only the teacher's own immediate satisfactions that are caught up in this process. In so far as professional success is judged by terminal examinations – and henceforward in England and Wales by a detailed and highly structured process of repeated pupil assessment as well – it is in the teacher's long-term interests to secure outcomes as favourable as possible. Both conscious and unconscious judgements will therefore lead to a concentration upon the successful education of those pupils most equipped to profit from an injection of cultural capital.

However, as stated above, the role of the pupil in education consumption is central. A good deal of the sociological literature of the past two decades has dealt with various aspects of pupil cultures, and the effects that they may be held to have upon the process of learning. One of the most influential studies in Britain was that carried out by Willis (1977). Examining the culture of male pupil resistance, he found that the ethos of the shop-floor provided the non-co-operative youths of his study with a basis for solidarity amongst themselves, in contradistinction to their more conformist peers, and also empowered them to see through and effectively to reject the types of learning transaction that the school culture was offering them – seeing these, in effect, as being for them as arbitrary and irrelevant as the imaginary examples based on surname initials or hair colouring that I proposed a few paragraphs ago.

This process of empowering, however, simultaneously deprives the youths in question of any likelihood of educational success, confirming their future destination as being that of the shop-floor with which they have already identified. In terms of social class reproduction, therefore, this empowering proves to have been a purely subjective phenomenon, rather than something that is transformative in terms of habitus, cultural capital, or economic potential for the individuals concerned.

Indeed, the point can be put more categorically and positively than this. Willis's argument is that this process is something that provides the dynamic for social class reproduction; schools, in this view, exist not only to generate new members of an élite, or new recruits to the numbers of technical functionaries, but also to produce future generations of the working class, whose 'failure' in the course of their schooling is therefore as necessary to this total outcome as is the 'success' of their co-operative classmates whom they so despise.

Apple (1979) put the point even more strongly, arguing (in an American context) that an unemployment rate of between 3 per cent and 6 per cent was in effect a necessity for the smooth running of the national economy, and that one of the functions of the schooling system was to contribute to the steady maintenance of this figure. The correspondence between the needs, at a macro-level, of the economy as a whole, and the effective outcomes of the schooling process, received their most influential examination in the work of Bowles and Gintis (1976), which also drew its data from an American context. Their depiction of the process of schooling showed it as being one which accustomed pupils to the experience of hierarchy, to the loss of control over, and ownership of, their work and its outcomes, and to the battle of all against all that was both enacted and symbolically represented by the habitual imposition of grading and testing exercises of various kinds.

The arguments I have summarized above relate to the universal experience of schooling, and as such have to do with questions of provision. However, Bowles and Gintis were also interested in matters of consumption; the experience of hierarchy, or of being tested, will of course be different according to whether pupils are on track for failure or success – whether they are learning to be managers or managed.

In the broad sweep of its argument, Bowles and Gintis's work is drawing a parallel (to put it no more strongly) between the demands of the economy and the workings of the schooling system. If the demands of the economy are seen as directly controlling the process of schooling by a kind of mechanical linkage, however, two problems arise. The first consists of the need to explain what are the precise couplings and fastenings which connect the demands to the processes, and this has always been very difficult for anyone not prepared to subscribe to a crude conspiracy theory. The second, for anyone working within a neo-Marxist frame of reference, is the embarrassment of being seen to keep improper company – in this case, that of the functionalists, whose notion of a system of checks and balances seemed designed to explain why things broadly stayed the same (just as a thermostat keeps a room temperature constant even when the thermometer dips outside) but whose vision of how things were, or might be, did not encompass the possibility, let alone the desirability, of revolutionary change.

In subsequent work (1988) Bowles and Gintis have gone some way towards safeguarding themselves against accusations of this kind. In particular, by paying some attention to the kinds of conflict that can occur – both within schools and between schools and other aspects of the wider economic system, such as the structure of the family or the capitalist mode of production – they have put some distance between themselves and the kind of smooth and untroubled harmony depicted by the functionalists.

It is certainly helpful to have these two categories of conflict identified and described. However, the more recognition is given to the relative autonomy of the school, or of the family, as against the wider workings of the state or of the economic system, the more a new set of problems piles up. For if, in the phrase 'relative autonomy', we emphasize the word *relative*, we are showing that in the end the economic system is still the motive power behind the actions and reactions we are considering. However, if we emphasize the word *autonomy*, we are in danger of suggesting that nothing in the end has all that much effect on anything else at all. And if we just leave the phrase to stand as an unanalysed oxymoron, we may not have produced an answer of any substantive value whatsoever.

It was for reasons like these that Lynch found it important to emphasize the particularism of consumption relations, as opposed to the universalism of provision relations, and in particular to highlight the role of mediating agencies, since to do so helps to overcome the ultimately vacuous and self-cancelling polarity expressed in the phrase 'relative autonomy'. After all, if a simple economistic model of the schooling process can be described as another example of the 'black box' approach – we know what goes in, and what comes out, but not what goes on inside – then a 'relatively autonomous' black box is a double mystery to us: we know neither what goes on inside it nor how its inputs and outputs relate to anything else; not only do we not see the inner workings, but we also find that we cannot see the connecting wires.

In the second chapter of this book I attempted to examine what we may now call some of the mediating practices carried out by the English teachers whose work was reported there. I drew particular attention to the way in which, consciously or unconsciously, they were developing and inculcating an ideology of quietism and conformity which has many of the characteristics of the hidden curriculum as discussed above. They themselves, I imagine, would not have represented their actions to themselves in this way, and might consciously have subscribed to very different ideals and goals. In doing so, they would have been sustained, to a greater or lesser extent, by their various reference groups: their departmental colleagues; their subject teaching peers, perhaps through the medium of a subject teaching association; more distantly, perhaps, the lecturers who had helped to develop their teaching styles during their professional training.

If we grant that all these individuals and groups were not consciously engaged in some monstrous conspiracy to do these pupils down, we have then, I would suggest, to accept that quietism and conformity constitute part of the hidden curriculum of schooling, and that the teaching of English, and particularly of literature, is tolerated or even encouraged, despite its lack of overt usefulness as a preparation for, or parallel to, the world outside school, because it fulfils this function. The same logic would also suggest that it would therefore only be replaced if a more effective means of achieving the same ends should be introduced.

To understand more completely, however, the place of English within the effective curriculum, we must consider where it is to be placed in terms of the classification into universalistic and particularistic practices. At a certain level, English teaching is the ideal example of a school subject which is universalistic in its provision, since it has traditionally been a compulsory subject in secondary schooling up to the age of sixteen, and its allotted role in the National Curriculum has confirmed it in this position. In consumption terms, however, it has varied a good deal, not only as a result of the various arrangements for streaming and setting that each school may have installed, and the variety of teaching styles that will have been generated by these and other means, but also as the outcome of a large number of other factors. In particular, the criteria that each school has adopted for the selection of examination candidates, the decision as to the particular examination to be undertaken (when the choice between GCE and CSE existed), and the further choice whether to enter pupils for a literature examination, all made significant differences to the kind of learning experiences that were on offer to pupils.

Furthermore, the consumption range is increased still further by the number of pupil cultures that can be brought to bear on the choices listed above, ranging from the kind of responses recorded by Willis, through a purely instrumental approach concerned with the acquisition of credentials, to an enthusiastic and wholehearted identification with the overt goals of the subject as they are declared by the teacher and others. If we were able to number and count these, they would then have to be multiplied by the number of routeways offered by the school, to give even the simplest and crudest picture of the types of consumption that might be experienced even within one particular institution.

The position is of course complicated still further if we consider the teaching of the subject at sixth-form level, as the third chapter of this book attempted to do. Here the pupils' attendance at school, and choice of subject, is entirely voluntary, the pupils' current acquisition of cultural capital and likely subsequent careers represent an orientation towards success, and the gratification experienced by the teacher on a minute-by-minute basis is at a maximum. Yet, as we have seen, the actual patterns of consumption vary enormously from pupil to pupil, and factors such as social origin, gender and ethnicity play a major part (as of course they do during the compulsory years of schooling also) in mapping out these patterns.

Jackson (1968) is usually credited as being the first person to have used the phrase 'the hidden curriculum'. His definition of it deals with the way in which the pattern of the school experience involves three elements: the experience of either delay or frustration in the fulfilment of pupils' wishes and intentions; the experience of obeying the commands of a person in authority which provides a kind of template for subsequent experience in the workplace; the experience of the dual and somewhat contradictory allegiance to both teacher and peer group that the school situation demands.

In the sixth-form setting, the experience of delay is reduced but is never entirely absent. The teacher, as we have seen, is still the person in authority; even if that authority is exercised in subtler ways, it is still necessary to learn how to respond to it, and to learn, for instance, that you have less control over the conversation if you are a girl. To this extent, it can be called only too effective a preparation for work, even if skilled and moderately valued work, in the world after school. Issues of allegiance to the peer group and to the teacher, as I have suggested, can be complicated by a convergence, in terms of underlying value and of certain aspects of conversational status, between the two.

In the particular context we have been looking at, it may indeed be necessary to collapse together the first two of Jackson's three categories. Delay can be seen as something relatively mechanical and external, such as the process of queuing outside a classroom door until the teacher permits entry. But it can also affect subtler aspects of behaviour, such as control of turns during the process of conversation as referred to above. We saw in Chapter 3 how the teacher reserved to herself the right to allocate turns in the discussion, even though it was clearly being conducted on the basis of considerable friendliness and affability. Yet this control ran parallel to an achieved convergence of values in the discussion of male bonding that the play precipitated.

Above all, though, it is necessary to remember that the pupils themselves are there in the classroom with considerably differing goals and agendas; it is only because they have such goals and agendas, indeed, that they are there at all, rather than at the local College of Further Education or in employment. Hashmat intends to read law at university; one of the boys is hoping to get a basketball scholarship to an American college. Quite apart from the differences in their experiences that arise from class, gender, and ethnicity, it would be surprising if the different forms of instrumentality that they bring to their classroom situation and experiences did not generate different forms of consumption.

So far in this chaper I have been treating Jackson's categories in the way in which they were intended to be used; that is to say, in relation to the overall processes of socialization to which pupils are exposed at school. Now, however, I want to try to see how far they may also be capable of being applied to the features that are specific to the subject matter of English teaching. In doing so, I should emphasize, I am at the least taking them a large step further than Jackson intended, and I am probably to some degree treating them as metaphorical rather than literal categorizations. However, I think they will survive the experience, and bring us some benefits in the process.

All works of literature – novels, certainly, but also frequently plays and poems too – are capable of deploying narrative as the basic organizing convention that they bring to bear on their selected material. It is easy to assent to such a proposition and then pass on, but before doing so it is worth pausing for a moment to consider just what is meant by 'narrative' in such a context. A definition which would command a considerable degree of agreement is that a narrative begins by outlining one state of affairs, then recounts an action that takes place, then outlines a new state of affairs that succeeds the first.

I have possibly just pulled off a sleight of hand in the sentence you have just read. You may perhaps be assuming that the action referred to was that which replaced the first state by the second state; however, that is not (if you look again) what the sentence is claiming. Barthes (1966, p. 94) calls this 'the confusion of consecution and consequence' and it is in general the kind of sloppy but generally fruitful thinking upon which we base both our understanding of written text and of a lot else in the experience of our daily lives. Indeed, in various important ways we may have learnt to apply such interpretative strategies to daily living because we first acquired some of them in listening to simple narratives:

Jack and Jill
Went up the hill
To fetch a pail of water.
Jack fell down
And broke his crown
And Jill came tumbling after.

The nursery rhyme succeeds in suggesting that not one but two accidents occurred as the result of the performance of what was once a normal domestic chore. Cause and effect, it should be noted, are never explicitly asserted. However it is not the overt information which counts here. Presumably the nursery rhyme was neither designed to suggest, nor succeeded in suggesting to most small hearers, that this was a necessary or even likely outcome of the performance of a domestic duty – any more than most of us will have been prompted to go looking for wells at the top, rather than the bottom, of hills by early and repeated exposure to the recitation of the verse.

What the rhyme does do, however, is to introduce to its hearers one of the basic patterns of daily experience: we all have to do things, sometimes we meet with misadventures in carrying them out, but mostly we survive and carry on. Though I call this a basic pattern, I do not mean to imply that there is something natural and inevitable about it; rather, it is something that we come to believe as the result of a powerful socializing process. After all, a critical reading of the rhyme could generate the learning of other messages, such as that it is dangerous to send unsupervised children to undertake tasks which they are not fully competent to perform. The reason that we normally extract the first moral rather than the second from the rhyme has a good deal to do with the learning context in which we meet it.

In introducing the basic concept of narrative I have done what most narratologists seem to do, which is to illustrate my points by a very short poem of one kind or another – frequently, indeed, the kind that I have chosen here. Obviously this is because of the economy of effort and space that can be achieved by citing them rather than complete novels or plays. It is of course possible to provide paraphrases of novels or plays that attempt to encapsulate their basic narrative structure. Newspapers and magazines of a literary persuasion seem, around Christmastime, to depend on them, offering small prizes to the person who can best cram the plot of *Hamlet* into fifty words. If this can be done (after a fashion) then it is worth posing a remarkably naïve question: why did Shakespeare bother to put all the other words in? If he had not, after all, his audience might have been able to get back home a lot earlier.

Presumably, however, they did not wish to get back home too early. In the same way the reader of a detective novel would feel cheated to discover on page two that the butler did it. So, although narrative works by progressing from state A to state B, the consumption of narrative typically requires that process to be disrupted, delayed, and sometimes suspended prior to final completion. Delay – the first of Jackson's categories – is therefore integral to the experience of reading and studying anything that has been produced in the narrative mode.

However, whereas the voluntary reader or member of the audience (in my examples above, the Jacobean theatregoer or the reader of detective novels) sees delay as something desirable, the same cannot always be said of the pupil who is set two chapters to read for homework. Habits of consumption can then incline towards rapid reading, selective reading, or any of the other strategies for rapid processing of text that we acquire as a sometimes unofficial, but severely practical, part of our battery of reading skills.

Moreover, the experience of delay is different for the theatregoer, who expects something like two hours' traffic on the stage, and the student of the same play for A level, who may anticipate spending a term or more on that same text. Narratologists like to compare narrating time (the 'pace' at which the storytelling runs) with narrated time (the time notionally taken by the events as they happened), but an at least equal contrast can be found between acting time and studying time. The pacing of this delay, of course, is primarily the responsibility of the teacher, who uses it to impart more and more information, or to generate more and more comment, concerning the work that is being studied. Just as the pacing of narrative, and the management of delay, within a novel is often the most obvious sign of a narrating voice or an authorial authority, so the pacing of learning within a sequence of lessons gives to a teacher an authority that is itself quasi-authorial. The authority of the narrative and the authority vested in the school system become mutually entangled and mutually supporting. It is, after all, the experience of nearly every pupil that, whereas it may be possible to slow a lesson down, it is quite impossible to speed it up.

What all of this means is that Jackson's second category, that of the submission to duty, is put into practice every time the pupil accedes or collaborates in the process of delay. The process is not, of course, one of brute repression, since the pupils themselves acquire greater status by becoming 'experts', and become slightly more akin to the teacher, by playing their roles in the transaction. In fact, the process is more readily compared to one of apprenticeship, in which the pupils progress through various stages in the acquisition of knowledge towards a future end-point, located somewhere after their final term, in which they themselves may acquire greater rights in respect of conversation management. Such at least is the promise that is implicitly held out to them; in practice, it is more likely that they are learning rules of conversational deference that the majority will be required to sustain throughout their working lives.

A further type of submission to duty, however – at least in my quasi-metaphorical sense of the term – relates to the relationship between pupil and set book. To begin with, the pupil typically has no control over what book is set. Even in those unusual cases where they are invited to participate in selection, it is a selection from a pre-established list, either set by a board of examiners, or determined by what is in the departmental store-cupboard. Indeed, in early planning for a national curriculum for English, it was envisaged that a list of books should be devised for nationwide use as at least a sort of benchmark for what pupils should be studying at any given time. Acceptance of allocated tasks is therefore something which pupils either internalize, or, by opposing in some way, experience as a barrier to future academic success and prospects of employment.

More fundamentally, acceptance of narrative, and all the values and assumptions that ride on the back of each narrative, is a form of submission to the disciplinary structure of the school. Since, within the format of a conventional lesson, no pupil can rewrite a canonical narrative, it constitutes a form of universalistic provision. Consumption can indeed be more variable: pupils can identify with the notion of a heritage, and in so doing reproduce the power relations that created it; they can accept it on an instrumental basis, with an identical result; they can resist or reject it, and in so doing label themselves as deviant or as failures of one kind or another. And, once they have submitted to the narrative, the values and assumptions can set to work, as I discuss elsewhere.

Duality of loyalty, the third of Jackson's aspects of the hidden curriculum, is the one that it is most difficult to illustrate by anything approaching empirical evidence, since the hidden aspects of pupil culture typically prove inaccessible to researchers unless, like Willis, they immerse themselves in the medium they are investigating. Nevertheless, in the sixth-form lesson that this book has looked at, there is some evidence of the successful management of this duality. In Chapter 3 I examined the way in which the culture of male solidarity was introduced, in part by the pupils themselves, into the lesson and then validated both by the use that was made by the teacher of the Shakespeare text and by the conversational negotiation between teacher and pupils. What we have here, however, is not so much duality as convergence on at least one aspect of a value system. Any parts of the male value system that could not undergo this process of convergence were kept out of the conversational frame. Indeed, the nearest that we came to any kind of overt disagreement was in the critical remarks offered by Hashmat on the question of female roles, and Hashmat, who is an advocate both of the emancipation of women and of arranged marriages, is managing, we may presume, a further set of cultural dualities of her own. Moreover, although the teacher neutralized Hashmat's challenge by not responding to its substance, she clearly expressed, during the lesson and afterwards in discussion, a considerable degree of fellow-feeling that seemed grounded, in part at least, on aspects of shared gender and class affiliation.

What I have tried to illustrate in this chapter is the way in which a hidden curriculum can work not only through such 'external' features as the control of time and space during the school day, but also 'internally' within the subject matter and pedagogy of English as it is constituted as a school subject. In particular, I have tried to suggest that narrative, as a thoroughly pervasive element in set texts of all descriptions, is a particularly effective bearer of this curriculum, since, like a roller coaster, once you have embarked on it you find that it is singularly difficult to get off or turn back.

The narrative mode is not of course confined to English lessons, and in one form or another it tends to turn up in most parts of the curriculum. In other school subjects, however, it is probably more susceptible to interrogation or independent verification; the pupils can see what colour the liquid turned in the test tube, or they have independent evidence as to which country lies on the opposite side of the English Channel. The fact that the narrative of a work of fiction is 'not true' makes it, paradoxically, even more effective, since there can be so little that is susceptible to an overt challenge. The everyday consumerist form of dissent – finding a book boring and abandoning it – is simply not available as an option to the school pupil. The skill of interrogating it in your own way has still to be discovered.

For this reason, it seems to me that a conscientious teacher of English has three very different and conflicting loyalties and duties. The first, which is generally recognized, is to interest and involve pupils as much as possible in the particular narratives that are being read or studied, both for the sake of that particular experience, and in order to develop the skills of reading and decoding narrative in general. The second consists of a responsibility to consider what effect that particular reading experience will have, not just in a generalized way, but at that particular time and in that particular classroom. This duty can be expressed in such areas as the selection of the reading material, and the control over the way in which it is taught. The third, I would suggest, is to show pupils various strategies with which to resist the tyranny of the text, to interrupt its smooth flow and ask awkward questions about what is being done by whom and to whom and why. After all, if the pedagogical experience is one of delay, and the narratological experience is one of deferral, then there is a kind of moral and political equity in enabling pupils to hold things up a little on their own account, and start asking just what this text, and this reading of this text, thinks it is doing.

8 The discipline of education

Unlike most other chapters of this book, this one takes as its starting point a set of issues which are seemingly a long way from the world of education. An examination of the training of an eighteenth-century Prussian soldier, or of changes in the treatment of the insane at the time of the French Revolution, can seem to have little or no bearing on what may have been going on in education, then or later. That they can plausibly be made to seem to have such a bearing is a tribute to the persuasiveness of the model of social processes that Foucault adopted, and, more particularly, to the way in which he proposed to investigate them.

Our principal means of knowing about changes that took place in social practices – often, our only means – is to study the documents which survive from the period, and Foucault points out we are accustomed to treating these as records of voices that are now silenced. An extremely naïve historian might conceivably be tempted to take them at their face value as evidence; more typically, a scholar would be aware that allowance had to be made for the ideological position from which they were written. Foucault regarded both these approaches as equally misguided, since both were grounded upon the error of treating the documents as 'traces' of lost voices, whereas for him they acquired significance only when compared and contrasted with other documents, so that a pattern might emerge. It is as though people had been looking for inscribed messages – treating them as microdots, perhaps – when all along the only way to make sense of the marks is to treat them as elements in a 'dot-to-dot' picture and join up the lines.

Denying the source documents the status of a record of a human voice is to adopt some kind of anti-humanist position, and this, together with what I have called Foucault's 'dot-to-dot' approach, accorded well with the anti-humanist features of the structuralism prevailing in Paris at the time, though Foucault was later to deny vigorously that he had ever been any kind of a structuralist. The name that he gave to his brand of analysis was 'archaeology', thereby emphasizing, as I see it, that he was not claiming any prior subjective knowledge of a culture, but was reconstructing its significant features from the patterns constructed and displayed by its artefacts. Moreover, and most importantly, what he was examining was not a collection of individual historical documents, but the discourses which generated them.

'Discourse' is always a slippery term to use, more abstract than 'speech' (*parole*), and more restricted than 'language' (*langue*). It can be thought of as being in some way the sum total of a set of documents or 'traces', or, more profitably, as the set of rules that must be satisfied before another can be included in their number. The most 'structuralist' way of using the term is to see it as generative of the utterances in question – a kind of linguistic Murphy's Law stating that if something can be made possible, then it is indeed likely to happen. What precisely this 'making possible' consists of, and who or what does the making, are questions to which it will be necessary to return.

The eighteenth century tends to be the pivotal period in Foucault's 'archaeological' explorations of changes in the organization and conceptualization of major public institutions; the way in which they were spoken about changed, and different things, seemingly, began to happen in them. During this period – though his focus is on the nature of the change in question, rather than the precise era in which it took place – he sees the administration of justice moving from the quasi-medieval imposition of savage and seemingly random exemplary punishments, to an ordered system of carceral institutions, in which imprisonment is construed as a penalty in itself, rather than as the means towards the exaction of some other penalty. He also detects a radical shift in the notion of the hospital, accompanied by a taxonomy of illnesses and their required treatments and also by a differentiation from other causes for institutionalization. Parallel with this went a whole assortment of other developments: a new understanding of what madness was, and what interventions might be possible; the creation of a modern, disciplined army; the rationalization of production in factories, in contrast to the relatively unstructured system of craft labour.

These changes in institutions were accompanied, as Foucault sees it, by revolutionary changes in the credentials required of those seeking the status of professionals qualified to treat or oversee these various conditions. Thus the forerunners of psychiatrists are differentiated from doctors professing general medicine. Doctors themselves are required to submit to examination, and to demonstrate requisite skills, as opposed to mere proof of attendance at the appropriate lectures. Professional status is thus achieved by means of a system of differentiation and inspection.

Most of the processes that Foucault is describing have usually been collectively depicted as one aspect of the general process known as the Enlightenment, in which a rational and largely secular form of social organization was seen as derived from the basis of a proper recognition of the rights of the individual. Foucault opposes this ameliorist interpretation of events, seeing them instead as the replacement of a randomized and undifferentiated form of subjugation by one that was more systematic but no more benign. Instead of recognizing a system constructed around the rights of individuals, Foucault saw a monstrous machine that, by obsessively incarcerating, ranking and classifying every bio-logical entity it encountered, was the main factor in constructing them as individuals. The incarcerated individuals were subject to the process of continu-ous observation discussed in Chapter 2 in connection with the scheme for the Panopticon. Their ascribed characteristics were entirely derived from the process that, in this sense, was responsible for their creation.

Horrific though Foucault's account of the Panopticon can seem, he never-theless omits some of its more bizarrely obsessive features. Thus it is central to his argument that 'character' (a term we tend to associate with the autonomous individual) is in fact exclusively a creation of the system. Yet one aspect of Bentham's proposals that Foucault, curiously enough, does not choose to cite is the suggestion, noted by Himmelfarb (1952), that the prisoners' designations and that of the institution should be chemically incised on their faces. This pathologically literal-minded version of 'labelling', in which the prisoner/patient/pupil is a *tabula rasa* subjected to institutional inscription, eventually becomes, appropriately enough, the subject matter of one of Kafka's more savage tales, *In the Penal Settlement* (1919).

The motive power behind this process of labelling and supervision is, in the profoundest sense, depersonalized. Foucault contrasts the *lettre de cachet* of the absolutist era, when the king, seated in public display, was the originator of the document that sent the victim to the darkest dungeon, with the reformed prison, in which the detainees are constantly visible, whereas the supervisors are hidden in the discreet anonymity of the central tower. Furthermore, the possi-bility exists that at any one time there may be nobody watching at all; all that matters is that the prisoners are obliged to behave in the light of the possibility that someone may be. 'He who is subjected to a field of visibility, and who knows it, assumes responsibility for the constraints of power; he makes them play spontaneously upon himself; he inscribes in himself the power relation in which he simultaneously plays both roles; he becomes the principle of his own subjection' (Foucault, 1977:202–3).

But, as was emphasized earlier, the warders are constituted by the process of observation just as much as are the prisoners, and are themselves subject to a complex process of review and assessment. The director of the institution silently monitors the work of his subordinates; in his absence, his family, friends, visitors, or servants can undertake the task. A visiting inspector can tell in a moment if all is properly in order. Furthermore, in the society that Bentham envisaged, it was the right of the general public to inspect the institution, and to determine if it was being well managed. The art of management, we can say, is thus simultaneously developed and deskilled; management assumes an ever more central role in the conduct of events, whilst the necessary skills are broken down and diffused throughout the system rather than being located and concentrated in the person of specific individuals. The Panopticon was an instrument not of tyranny but of democracy, in which all the employees are accountable to those outside. Thus even the director is the object of viewing, as well as a viewer, and is subjected, by and through his own actions, to the effects of a depersonalized power. Appropriately enough, in Kafka's tale also the officer from the penal colony finally imposes on himself the punishment he has spent a lifetime meting out to others.

In something of the same spirit, doctors and other professionals are monitored and regulated, so that they themselves are as much 'servants of the system' as the lowliest patient for whose well-being they have responsibility. And, though I will not itemize all Foucault's evidence and assertions here, his overriding point is that the process outlined above is not one that is unique to the prison system, but can be paralleled in the army, in welfare institutions, in the factory system, and throughout the social fabric. Seen in this light, therefore, the 'Enlightenment' is then more like some incomprehensible and irreversible calamity, a kind of fallen state that cannot be attributed to anything as precisely identifiable as the eating of a forbidden fruit.

The summary that I have just offered above does scant justice to a complex and substantial body of work. More particularly, it offers categorical statements where Foucault himself had recourse to elaboration, paradox, and a tantalizing form of evasion when confronted, by interviewers or by the logic of his own argument, with the temptation to offer a blunt assertion. What I want to do, however, is to develop some means of applying this depiction of a general process to the development of an understanding of the particular processes involved in English teaching.

From what I have described above, it should be relatively simple to see how Foucault's analysis can be extended to the functioning of schooling in England and Wales. Indeed, Foucault himself draws some of his examples from the work of Lancaster and Bell, and provides an analysis of the monitorial system that closely parallels the one I have paraphrased above concerning the working of prisons. There are, however, two dissimilarities between what he generally writes about on the one hand, and educational history on this side of the Channel on the other, that I will mention only to set aside. The first is the observation that the development of a universal and compulsory system of schooling came much later here than did the universalizing reforms of Napoleon. So indeed did a number of other reforms, such as the abolition of the practice of purchasing commissions in the army. This is true but irrelevant; it is no part of Foucault's argument that he is describing the spirit of one particular age. The second is that many of his instances are drawn from total institutions – a national army or whatever. It is easy to believe that the sheer diversity of educational provision in this country, coupled with the fact that its compulsory nature is of such very recent provenance, safeguards us from the kind of megalomaniac horrors that Foucault depicts so graphically. But it is no part of Foucault's case that a phenomenon has to be universal before it is effective; so long as an institution functions in the way he describes, and creates the forms of behaviour that he has outlined, it qualifies as one of his carceral institutions, no matter how much diversity, plurality, and laxity there may be outside it.

The first feature of a carceral institution is its overwhelming attention to the arrangement of detail. Thus, in the reformed Prussian Army of the eighteenth century, it was specified that during the moves to be carried out in the course of parade-ground drill there were to be 'six stages to bring the weapon to one's foot, four to extend it, thirteen to raise it to the shoulder etc.' (p. 154). This kind of obsessive analysis of synergy into its component parts, if exhibited in most other contexts, would raise serious doubts about the analyst's sanity. In a carceral institution, however, it is essential to the functioning of the whole, subordinating the individual will to the patterns of joint behaviour, and creating a kind of new composite military body that is more powerful in its functioning than the sum of any number of individual forays.

But this compulsive categorization is not unique to the army. Foucault cites (pp. 159–60) a French work on education, Demia's *Règlement pour les Écoles de la Ville de Lyon*, dating from 1716, which categorizes seven levels in the process of learning to read. These range from those pupils who are beginning to learn their letters, through those who can join syllables together to make words, to those in the top grade who can read manuscripts. However, each level is also capable of being subdivided: the first into those who are learning 'simple letters', those learning 'mixed' letters, those learning 'abbreviated' letters (â, ê, etc.), and those on 'double' letters (ff, ss, etc.). Each subsequent level is also subdivided in a similar way. The intention is that this classification should form the basis for school classes, and for setting within them. The possibilities that this system offers for detailed management and control, steering each pupil through a system via the approval of a teacher's inspection, are what drew Foucault's attention to the text.

One wonders, therefore, what he would have made of a system of ten levels of reading ability, each subdivided into between four and six items, ranging from 'Begin to recognize individual words or letters in familiar contexts' through 'Read silently and with sustained concentration' to 'Recognize, in discussion, whether subject matter in non-literary and media texts is presented as fact or as opinion', the whole ensemble constituting only one of three components of a subject that in turn is one amongst many within the curriculum. All my examples are taken from the English proposals for ages 5 to 16. One feels Foucault would have been impressed by the meticulous organization of temporal progression, by the continuous surveillance that such a system necessarily entails, and by the individualized profiling that results from the activity.

For it was Foucault's argument that in many societies, of which feudal society can stand as an example, individualization attached only to the powerful and the eminent – everyone knew who the king was, what kind of character he was supposed to have, and what his face looked like on the coinage – whilst the great mass of the people remained undifferentiated, since 'ordinary individuality . . . remained below the threshold of description' (p. 191). In a 'disciplinary' society, however, such as we are more familiar with from our daily experience, the powerful become more and more anonymous (how many pupils can name the

Secretary of State who introduced the 1988 Act?) whilst 'the child is more individualized than the adult, the patient more than the healthy man, the madman and the delinquent more than the normal and the non-delinquent' (p. 193). In effect, Foucault is rephrasing the point I summarized earlier concerning the invisibility of the supervisor and the visibility of his subjects.

The kind of detailed classification of pupils that Foucault is describing is only feasible if sustained and nourished by frequent testing and examination. It is important, in Foucault's scheme of things, to remember that testing is a two-way procedure. The fact that it is to occur is a guarantee that the teacher, for self-interested reasons if for no other, will use every endeavour to transmit knowledge to the pupils. As it occurs, it generates a knowledge about the pupils that is transmitted to the teacher. This system contrasts with the medieval principle of the masterwork, which merely recorded the fact that the transmission of knowledge and skill had already taken place, without individualizing or differentiating the apprentice, or indeed classifying his performance on anything other than a pass/fail basis. The master, too, remained a relatively anonymous figure, his teaching skills uncategorized and unattended to.

It is therefore possible to compare a terminal examination, such as was the GCE, with at least certain aspects of the medieval apprenticeship system, since it aimed to be a once-for-all testing of a completed process of learning. Cumulative forms of assessment, such as the CSE Mode 3, and more particularly the GCSE examination, are already moving towards the pattern preferred by the Brothers of the Christian Schools who, in the late eighteenth century, wanted their pupils examined daily, with spelling on the first day of each week, handwriting on the afternoon of the third day, and so on. Superimposed on this weekly pattern, there was to be a monthly examination to determine those whose work was to be seen by the inspector (p. 186). Such an inspection, of course, contributes to the assessment of the teacher as well as that of the pupils; the teacher in a disciplinary society is subjected to considerable analysis and description, and it is perhaps not surprising if the introduction of pupil assessment in the late eighties should be smartly followed by that of teacher appraisal in the early nineties.

The system of examination, and the expectations that attended on it, Foucault saw as being at once tolerant and prescriptive, investigative and normative in their functioning. We can compare the reformed system of military drill, which was at once expressive and generative of a higher power, and at the same time grounded on an understanding of the articulation of the human body and what was ergonomically feasible for it to perform. In the same way, the children of the Christian Schools were never to be placed in a lesson for which they so far lacked the capacity, since they would then fail to learn anything, yet it was expected that they would complete their learning within a stipulated time, and they were exposed to derision if they did not do so.

With all of this we can compare the instructions for the conduct of assessment of reading that are contained in English Proposals 5 to 16, para. 16.45 to 16.53. Assessment is to be both internal and external, and is to be moderated. Internal assessment is to be continuous, and based on structured observation by the teacher. External assessment, generally conducted by the teacher, should be fit for the purpose, and rewarding and enjoyable for the pupils. A common national format for record-keeping is to be devised and used. The tests should take account not only of reading skills but also of such factors as the child's reading tastes and preferences. Testing should arise naturally out of good classroom practice, and the test questions should be what experienced teachers would be likely to ask. Marking should distinguish 'positive' errors from 'negative' ones. The results of testing should be able to be used formatively, and can cue in either further diagnostic testing or a programme of enrichment.

Most of these recommendations can be taken as liberal and positive developments, and it may be thought that I am being churlish not to join in the general chorus of welcome that they received. However, I want to compare them with Foucault's account of what it is that the process of training in a disciplinary society consists of. Drawing his examples once more from the eighteenth-century training of soldiers, he speaks of four principles. According to the first, time is divided into units of definite duration, within which specific skills are to be taught according to the level of advancement achieved by each subject. The second specifies that simple elements should be combined into a totality of increasing complexity. The third prescribes examinations at the end of each stage, which both ensure that the subjects have reached the same stage and differentiate their performance at this point. The fourth and key point laid down that there should be a branching programme of future development, varying according to the rank and advancement of each individual. The parallel seems almost uncannily close.

When discussing the application of this type of disciplinary regime to schooling, Foucault points out that its reference points are both natural and normative, or, in his terms, involve 'a double juridico-natural reference' (p. 179). School regulations laid down that pupils should not be prescribed work that was too difficult for them to undertake, since they would learn nothing from the experience. The pace of learning was therefore grounded on the nature of the pupil, just as the military drill was grounded upon the articulation and co-ordination of the human body. At the same time, pupils' persistent failure at set tasks would expose them to public opprobrium as a form of corrective punishment. The stated intention of the National Curriculum, with its public attribution of degrees of success or failure in collective performance to each different school, is to apply this form of punishment at an institutional level; it remains to be seen how far it may in practice come to operate at an individual level as well.

For Foucault, punishment can be seen as fulfilling five functions simultaneously, though each logically proceeds from the one before. The first refers the individual to the collective norm for the purposes of comparison. The second differentiates individuals one from another on the basis of this comparison. The third constructs a hierarchy of value into which individuals are to be inserted on the strength of this differentiation. The fourth inculcates a conformity arising out of a wish to progress within the hierarchy. The fifth differentiates those who are 'normal' and enclosed within this system from the 'abnormal', who are defined by the system but excluded, suspended, or in some way bracketed off. In summary, then, disciplinary power 'compares, differentiates, hierarchizes, homogenizes, excludes' (p. 183).

I suggested above that Foucault's concept of 'discipline' was capable of being applied both to human individuals and to collective institutions such as schools, since both constitute 'subjects', and both are 'subjected' to the disciplinary process. This may seem to many people an unfamiliar use of the term 'subject', but the concept it expresses is by no means unique to Foucault; I was intrigued to discover recently that Christian charismatics hold that possession by devils can afflict not only individual sinners, but also such corporate entities as commercial companies. Foucault, however, has no service of exorcism that he can offer us, and his version of reality can at times seem terminally pessimistic in that it offers little in the way of means of escape from, or even alteration of, the social energies it so graphically describes.

Such pessimism may seem at odds with some of Foucault's comments I have quoted earlier to the effect that the exercise of power is also generative of resistance, so that power and resistance grow together like a couple of climbing plants. However, there is in the end little comfort to be derived from this concept. Just as the process of supervision in the Panopticon both defined and confined both the prisoners and their observers, so the effects of resistance can conspire with the effects of power towards a common goal. The best metaphor I can offer here is that of a death in a quicksand, in which the suffocation of the unfortunate victim is the outcome both of the suction power of the viscous medium, and of the captive's desperate struggles to escape from it.

However, metaphors form a kind of quicksand of their own, and it is perhaps advisable to move on to firmer ground. I have briefly looked at what, in Foucault's definition, power consisted of, but there are other questions to be asked, such as where it came from, and what it was there to do. On these points Foucault is frequently evasive, though within the terms provided by his own definitions he can perhaps claim that these are improper questions. However, the rapid somersault from an absolutist to a disciplinary society is, by most people's standards, a major change, and it is difficult not to feel that the lack of a satisfactory explanation for the motive force behind such a major change – and the lack of any strong and apparent wish to discover such an explanation – are two of the more valid criticisms that have been laid at Foucault's door.

In the place of these absent explanations, Foucault offers us a definition instead. But let us first see what some explanations would look like. A liberal history of the development of schooling would emphasize the role of reformist individuals, their concern for the welfare and development of the common masses, and the gradual, if inexorable, triumph of their rational arguments over traditional sloth and bureaucratic obstruction. Milestones on this path would be the introduction of universally compulsory education in 1870, of secondary education for all in 1944, and of comprehensive education, principally in the period from the 1960s to the present day. Within English teaching, a parallel progress would be traced from the not-too-distant days when it did not take place at all, through the various phases of subordination to state imperatives, to the point at which the development of the individual consciousness became all-important.

As against this, a Marxist explanation would insist that progress was not so even, nor motives so patent, or indeed, at a purely individual level, so relevant. The development of schooling would be related to the requirements of the economy for more skilled labour during a period of economic expansion and imperial aggrandizement. Within English teaching, the inculcation of national values, of communicative skills, or of a belief in individual development would be seen as amounting to little more than ideological phenomena, whose relationship to underlying realities remained to be teased out by analysis. Discussion within Marxism might centre on whether these phenomena were entirely driven by the interaction of political and economic forces, or whether the phenomena themselves might have an effect on other aspects of the social fabric.

These are patently two very different types of explanation. What they have in common, however, is that they both assume the intervention of some kind of an agency, acting within the continuum of historical change, and producing consequences that redound to the advantage of some definable social group. Each explanation can, in different ways and to different degrees, be subjected to empirical testing of some kind or other.

Foucault, however, rejects the notion of agency, at least in the way in which I have described it above. It is not the case that a new type of prison regime is advocated by a reformer, or that a government wills a new pattern to educational provision, or that changes in relations of production and distribution are reflected in cultural phenomena. Or, if such is the case, then these are coincidences or consequences, but not causes. First it is one way, then it is another way, and a new form of discourse has come into being. All else ensues from this.

But let us consider one particular case – that of the proposals for the Panopticon, which have formed so much of a running theme throughout this book. A brutally literal-minded critic might be tempted to comment that, since the building was never constructed, the whole business is 'only' discourse anyway, and nothing to do with reality. An empirically-minded commentator might suggest that, since the examples that Foucault calls in evidence are so various in their chronology, what he has done is to reify and even fetishize his own particular notion of an epoch – an irregular and uneven slice cut across the chronology of history. A cynic might note that, as Gertrude Himmelfarb's helpful study (1952) spells out for us, Bentham envisaged making a tidy fortune by contracting to build and supervise the prison himself, and even abandoned his fundamental objection to association between prisoners once an architect pointed out how much cheaper it would be not to have so many party walls.

Whether or not Foucault was himself of the opinion that he had fetishized the notion of an epoch, he gradually moved away from the type of analysis provided by his early 'archaeological' works such as *Discipline and Punish* in the direction of more 'genealogical' writings. The term is taken from Nietzsche, and it is in a Nietzschean vein that he came to speak of another phenomenon which he labelled 'power/knowledge' to indicate that there is no such thing as a disinterested exercise in cognition; all knowledge, all systems of thought, all mechanisms for the inculcation of knowledge or belief are instances of power in action. Conversely, he claimed that there can be no exercise of power without some corresponding cognitive manifestation.

For our purposes, therefore, we have to ask how monolithic a phenomenon power/knowledge has proved to be. There are dangers at either end of the scale. If it simply means that there are innumerable forms of discourse, each of which packs a micropolitical punch, then it is too weak a phenomenon to have much explanatory force. If, at the opposite extreme, it is to be taken as a single and all-pervasive phenomenon, perhaps a bit like Cobbett's notion of The Thing which was to be detected conspiring against all good men everywhere, then it has to be regarded, in the end, as too simplistic a piece of anti-authoritarianism.

It should be said at once that this last position was a long way from Foucault's own. Typically, as he sees it, there are to be found in play in any one context a number of different discourses, many if not all of which contain mutually contradictory elements. It is as a result of such overlaps and discontinuities that the intertwining opposition of power and resistance comes to be played out at the level of discourse.

Since education is a critical site for the playing-out of conflict between discourses, and since English lessons, as we have seen, are a particularly sensitive area in which to observe this conflict, it is important to establish, as the conclusion of this chapter, just what forms of opposition can be observed there, and just what Foucault can tell us about them. In order to focus on one particular aspect of this, it will be helpful to re-examine Foucault's summary of disciplinary power, which 'compares, differentiates, hierarchizes, homogenizes, excludes' (p. 183).

The exclusion to which he refers does not mean that a subject or a concept simply vanishes in order to reappear in another discourse, or in some other way vanishes off the map. To take an example, consider the process that was involved (at least in the worst imaginable educational setting in the recent past) in labelling a boy as educationally subnormal. It neither meant that he would thenceforth receive no education, nor implied that he would cease to be categorized in educational terms. On the contrary, the pupil would be compared with 'normal' pupils (and the score in English deemed highly significant in this regard), found to be different, considered to be worse, encouraged to do better, and removed to a different institution at least until this process (we would all be expected devoutly to hope) had been completed.

Now contrast that little story with another (set this time in the 1990s) in which the pupil, despite extremely poor scores in English and various other subjects, shows brilliance in playing a musical instrument, and is awarded a scholarship to an independent school that specializes in musical tuition. Again the discourse into which the pupil now moves is an educational one, but it is clearly a different discourse, and the criteria for the evaluation of the pupil are different ones. In the first school, musical enthusiasm (as shown, let us say, in surreptitious listening to a personal stereo) represents resistance; in the second, musical ability provides access to power.

This little tale can be developed in a number of ways; even as it stands, it poses a number of interesting questions for us. What, for instance, will the school staff say around the time of the pupil's departure – how will they manage the co-presence of different educational discourses? How will the pupil respond in the new school when power is realized via musical performance, rather than by more conventional academic achievement? What form might resistance take in such a school? Yet perhaps we should not overstate the difference between the two educational settings and educational discourses; after all, there exist other discourses, such as those to do with the obtaining of employment, which will have little trouble in dealing with and comparing the two milieux.

One other point should be noted at this stage. 'Discourse' as used in the paragraphs above refers not just to the words that are uttered, or the concepts that are in play, but includes also the apparatus of testing and categorization. Since the National Curriculum will apply to the first school but not to the second, we are clearly looking at two significantly different disciplinary procedures. And, since power in Foucault is positive and constitutive, not just negative and prohibitive, it may well produce in this instance an instrumental virtuoso who will come to play a major role in the musical world.

What I have been looking at here is a hypothetical instance, though one that surely has many close parallels in the real world. We have, however, already seen examples from that world, as when, in Chapter 3, we looked at the intersection of the discourses of literature teaching and of extra-scholastic male bonding. In fact, in the case of the pupil heading for a basketball scholarship, we had an example that was very close indeed to my present, imaginary, one. But we had one even closer to Foucault's concerns, in Hashmat's attempts to introduce a discourse that analysed and commented on the repression of women. In an interview originally conducted in 1977 (Foucault, 1980a) we are told that school discipline is significant in that it is one of the key ways in which power gains access to, and then 'incorporates' (the pun is deliberate) the bodies of individuals, as part of its positive and constitutive force. This is not just a question of individuals, however, since it is of a piece with the accumulation of capital; the accumulation of a labour force is part of the same process. So the technologies of power have to cope with the management of humanity as a mass. Foucault declares:

> I believe that the political significance of the problem of sex is due to the fact that sex is located at the point of intersection of the discipline of the body and the control of the population. (p. 125)

It is important to understand here that, though sex is never simple, it was a matter of particular complexity for Foucault, who was eventually to produce a three-volume history of the subject. It would be intrepid of me to attempt to summarize it here, but fortunately Foucault has performed this task for me in the interview from which I quoted above. As with other issues, Foucault stresses that sex is not just something that is natural and given; rather, it is an outcome of discourse, constructed and given as a set of possible roles and patterns of behaviour, which individuals can accept or struggle with, but which they cannot jettison.

As with other changes that occurred in the eighteenth century, Foucault sees the discourse of sex as something that, for the first time, links the personal and the general in a new and special way, so that campaigns against masturbation are part of the same discourse as questions of public health and hygiene. This is what Foucault means by the 'intersection of the discipline of the body and the control of the population'. But, if he is right, then this underscores what others, writing from different perspectives, have nevertheless said anyway, which is that the meanings of sexual roles and sexual relationships in, to take our present example, the text of a Shakespeare play would be understood markedly different-ly by an original and by a present-day audience or readership.

In this case, it could be said that Hashmat is making an anachronistic error in supposing that comments derived from her understanding of present-day sexual roles can be read back into an interpretation of a play written some four centuries earlier. Against this, however, she would be entitled to offer two counter-arguments. One, to the effect that patriarchy is absolutely or virtually transhistorical, would take her outside the scope of possible agreement with Foucault. The other, that what she is reading is not a play written a long time ago, but something which is, for her, contemporary, since that is the only way in which we can read literature, raises questions that Foucault would be happy to discuss.

He did in fact discuss some of the issues relating to authorship and authority in an essay entitled 'What is an Author?' (1979). Amongst the interesting points he raises there is the notion that the work of literature, intrinsically capable of giving rise to a variety of meanings, is in fact limited and circumscribed by having an author's name attached to it, since:

> the name seems always to be present, marking off the edges of the text, revealing, or at least characterizing, its mode of being. The author's name manifests the appearance of a certain discursive set and indicates the status of this discourse within a society and a culture. (p. 147)

Another way of putting this is to say that there is a circularity of argument in the definitions that are conventionally and unthinkingly applied. Shakespeare wrote Shakespearean plays, which are the kind of plays which were written by Shakespeare. Foucault traces two different roots for this kind of thinking. The first is to be found in Christian exegesis, in which patristic scholarship is concerned to establish the authenticity of texts, and sets about doing so by deploying various internal and external forms of comparison. The other, which is of more immediate interest to us here, relates once more to practices in the eighteenth century.

At that point the author's involvement in the discourse he had produced, which had hitherto been chiefly penal (he could, for instance, be punished for blasphemy) acquired, to the full extent that we now recognize as normal, the characteristics of having rights of property over his production. This involved, of course, a number of legal changes: copyright laws, contracts between author and publisher, attribution of the status of goods to literary works, and so on. This codification, it should by now be unnecessary to stress, takes place in parallel with the other changes in social ordering that Foucault has identified as occurring at or around this period.

What Foucault does not particularly draw out, however, is the way in which the codification and specification of sexual norms and sexual deviations parallels, not only historically but also homologically, the allocation of legal rights and responsibilities to authors. Just as the role of sexual deviant is made available to individuals (whereas the previous discourse had conceived only of deviant acts committed by undifferentiated individuals) so authors, being inserted into an apparatus of control and discipline, of individuation and observation, can become transgressive in a way that was not previously possible. So Shakespeare is both, so to speak, a signature attached to a number of play texts, and by a kind of back-attribution an author who may be interrogated and judged.

Interrogation and judgement thus become the dominant modes of literary discussion in classrooms and in all other contexts into which this particular discourse can penetrate. But, whilst the pupils in the class are interrogating and judging the text, they are themselves the objects of interrogation and judgement. A double process of observation and differentiation is under way. And since the texts that they study are characteristically concerned with normative and deviant sexual roles, the discourse of sexuality becomes, not for the first time, intertwined with the discourse of education. If a body of literature addresses this problematic, and if a school subject offers to deal with this literature, then this particular intersection of the personal and the political, of control over the body and control over the workforce, is likely to continue to be the crucible of the curriculum.

9 The constitution of English

This book has not been written in a narrative mode, but, even so, readers could be forgiven for thinking that two characters in it, Bakhtin and Foucault, have been popping in and out of the plot like erring or outraged husbands in a French farce. Perhaps it is time to allow them to meet. What is most likely to bring them together is a discussion of the differing ways in which they depict action and counter-action, word and counter-word, in the continuous but by no means seamless process for which conversation will, for the moment, have to stand as the relatively neutral signification.

And yet perhaps that meeting may be a mistake. I suggested earlier that often they were both great system builders who seemed congenitally incapable of achieving a finished system; perhaps, even, this is because they would become dissatisfied with it as soon as it was completed. To forestall such a possibility, they would intermittently upset the balance of their own architectural creations by throwing out a new wing or adding an ornamental turret. If the fundamental image of language variation is still that of the Tower of Babel, then Bakhtin is the kind of builder who would pre-empt the divine wrath by asking in the tribes and dialects and rejoicing in the babble that ensued. And we do not have to resort to metaphor in the case of Foucault, since from time to time he speculated on what would happen if the prisoners took over the Panopticon, and what goals they would then set for themselves.

For all that, the Panopticon, considered both as a historical proposal by Bentham and as an image of social processes espoused by Foucault, is an abstractly schematic affair. Bentham first banished conversation, and then, permitting it in his later versions of the plan, with the naïveté that seems to lurk at the heart of many megalomaniacs, assumed that it would be anodyne. Foucault, more realistically, acknowledged that the language of power would intertwine with the language of resistance, but in the end saw them as just two sides of the same coin. To be sure, anyone who has visited a prison, even for half an hour, cannot fail to be aware of the rich sociolinguistic mix to be found there. This is not just a matter of accent and dialect, but of the accommodations, compromises, and petty conspiracies that flourish in such a setting, and are mediated and achieved through a variety of skilful uses of language. Since some of these conspiracies are apparently oppositional in nature, but, globally, enable the system to survive (the drug culture of the prison system would be a case in point; officially frowned upon, yet tacitly permitted in order to neutralize revolt) it could be argued that this is indeed an example of the imbrication of power and resistance in the way that Foucault outlined. Yet this argument, pushed too far, would turn Foucault into the kind of functionalist thinker, finding ways in which a use of language subordinately preserves the status quo, that would be a travesty of his actual position. For he held both that language use (or, rather, discourse in his particular use of this term) was constitutive of power structures, conceptual categories, and human relationships, and that discourse involved more than the use of words, but was part of a package of social forces. If, therefore, the prisoners were to take over the prison, they would have to find from somewhere a new way of talking and a new way of being for the new situation to be more than a mirror-image of the original one. Where this new discourse was to come from remained unclear.

Foucault would also, I imagine, be happy to agree that any one discourse is not completely monolithic, even if he would feel obliged to add that discourses in a disciplinary society all share certain features with one another. My own experience of prisons consists of tutoring undergraduates in them. These students have always commented on their sense of the contrast between the language they use in tutorials and that which they deploy in the rest of their prison life. One astutely remarked that university study was his own preferred drug. My own feeling, as I marked and commented on his work as one small part of a programme of continuous assessment for academic purposes that was likely to last as long as his sentence, was that my role in one disciplinary system was uncomfortably like that of the warder in the corridor outside in respect of another discursive formation.

Mention of the minutiae of continuous assessment serves to remind us of another of Foucault's defining features of a disciplinary society, which is that it will characteristically use a laicized version of religious codes of discipline so as to generate power and control in and through the observance of this code. In the case of a prison, the Home Office regulations fulfil this function, and it is worth noting in passing that both monks and prisoners occupy cells. Just as the Rule of St Benedict codified the behaviour of the religious in a closed and gathered community, curtailing the sometimes anarchic freedom of hermits in their scattered dwellings, so post-Enlightenment prisons, removing the prisoners from solitary oubliettes and treating them more humanely, can be said to control their actions and thoughts more comprehensively by dint of doing so.

The process inevitably operates somewhat differently in schools, since pupils virtually by definition are to be found there in the mass rather than individually. Perhaps, though, Foucault's perceptions can still serve us if we shift the level of observation, and consider both school departments and schools as if they were individuals. In such a case there is a dual process to be observed. Legislation over the past 120 years has served to standardize certain features of education, whilst inspection, both formal and informal, differentiates and hierarchizes the particular institutions, and, in extreme cases, has excluded some as well. More recently, the legislation of the eighties has worked to increase the differentiation and individuation of schools in two ways. The first, operating at the level of formal management, has increased the number of types of institution, each of which is intended to take its place in a hierarchy of esteem. The second, by means of the continuous process of monitoring and observation that the National Curriculum represents, ensures the ranking of each school within the category to which it belongs, and relevant legislation envisages the closure of the least popular. Seen in this light, the proliferation of detail entailed in the National Curriculum has to be considered not as an unfortunate excess of zeal but as its entire point, since it is only through imposing continuous and minute examination that the gaze of disciplinary observation can function. Moreover, since observation has to be seen to be both continuous and comparative to be effective, Kenneth Clarke is perfectly logical in his insistence that assessment has to be based on written and not oral work.

At the level of the English department, as much of this book has attempted to show, different discourses are to be found even within the confines of a single document. Kingman's reference to 'the powerful and splendid history of the best that has been thought and said in our language' (p. 11) is of a very different order from 'talk is not merely social and communicative, it is a tool for learning' (p. 43), and both are different from 'Competence in language is essential to competence in any job' (p. 7). The first genuflects towards the notion of cultural heritage, the second underscores a humanist commitment to a process of growth and development with no immediate practical outcomes, and the third yields to an ultimately economistic understanding of the value of communicative competence.

Part of the work of any analyst is therefore to show that these different ideologies, or forms of language use, or discourses, or whatever they may be, are in fact different one from another, and capable of resonating differently with different members of a department, or perhaps even with the same person at different times. But another and perhaps overriding task may be to examine whether, despite these genuine differences, they are co-factors working together within a specific historical context to have a certain effectivity that they would not have at other times or in other places. For this to be so, words alone can no longer be the sole subject matter, since we have to consider them in conjunction with legislation and its effects, with shifts in public attitude and perception, and with anything else that we may consider falls within the proper scope of a discursive formation.

It is for this reason that I find it useful to suggest both that the documents relating to the development of English within the National Curriculum contain surprisingly progressive and egalitarian elements, and that, taken in conjunction with the rest of the National Curriculum, they contribute towards the expansion of the kind of disciplinary society that Foucault outlined. What in effect they achieve, despite a certain amount of token recognition, is the jettisoning of the cultural heritage model that formed a kind of undercurrent or residue even in documents such as the Bullock Report. Since a cultural heritage is something that, considered in its own terms, you either have or have not, it is not susceptible to the kind of monitoring and inspection that Foucault's disciplinary processes depend upon. English teachers, accustomed to charges of lack of objective criteria when marking literature essays, have always been only too aware of this as a nagging professional issue. On the other hand, a skills-based approach lends itself remarkably readily to inspection, and requires only that a table of the requisite skills be prepared. Personal growth is altogether more of a borderline case: if it is seen as a progression through some pre-ordained series of stages (as, for example, in Piaget's psychology) then it is open to inspection of a kind, even if the process of inspection requires considerable tact and skill. But if growth is invisible to the external observer, and if it proceeds unpredictably in a number of different and non-quantifiable directions, then it is a less favourable vehicle. This being so, it is perhaps not surprising that Kingman was concerned to identify and promulgate a model of the English language which, whatever its limitations in the eyes of people whose primary interest is in linguistics, does provide the necessary sequencing and staging for the disciplinary gaze to take place.

Furthermore, Professor Henry Widdowson, in his Note of Reservation at the end of the Report, was both right and wrong in declaring that Kingman never made clear 'what English is on the Curriculum *for*' (p. 77), and in pointing out (p. 78) that there is a logical disjuncture in the Report between conceptions of child development within schooling and conceptions of adult need that are entertained in the wider world. In the same way, it is never made clear within military training manuals (such as those that Foucault discussed) what purpose is served by parade-ground drills, and the demands of military discipline do not always neatly correlate, at a purely rational and overt level, with those of the social forces they exist to sustain. What Widdowson and others are looking for (quite properly, at the level of intellectual debate) is a rationale; what is provided instead is a homology.

Since English has usually been seen as a humanistic discipline, it is understandably highly uncongenial to many of its most committed practitioners to be invited to see individuals or institutions as being constituted in the way that Foucault describes. This is because the mode of formation, from the outside inwards, is so contrary to the type of organic metaphor that is central to so much English thinking. Being so contrary, it can then lead to the unwarranted assumption that it implies also a high (or perhaps absolute) degree of determination. What I want to do in the rest of this chapter is to see how far this assumption is a necessary one.

What Bakhtin shares with Foucault is this perception that humans are built from the outside inwards, and that this building takes place in and through language. Where he has a different emphasis from Foucault is in having a very lively sense that this process of building is never complete, and continues, practically second by second, at a kind of micro-level of language use. The nature of the individual human being is therefore unstable on a temporal dimension in at least two different fashions. One of these relates to the way in which we engage with others in conversation, and in so doing lay ourselves open to the possibilities of change as a result of that conversation. The other relates to the kind of planning we carry out in the process of speech, responding to what others have just said to us, and anticipating what we expect will be their response to the utterance we are in the process of formulating.

The idea that people change through time and through engaging in conversation poses no problem for people with humanist preconceptions, since it is in keeping with the general organicist assumption of growth and progression. What is more worrying for them is the notion that our conversation – the very utterance we produce, and at the moment we speak them – is not our own, but is shot through with others' meanings and intentions. This is something much more threatening than the generally accepted idea that language is common property, whereas messages or utterances are the property of the individual. People are happy, so to speak, to accept the idea that the telephone company owns the wires, but get alarmed if they suspect that it has taken out copyright on the conversations – especially those that have not yet taken place.

Bakhtin's recurring emphasis on utterance rather than language as the subject for investigation is capable of being read (at least through half-shut eyes) as affirming the individual ownership of the utterance in contrast to the common ownership of the language system. On the basis of the reading, frequent attempts have been made to recruit him as a covert liberal, sending messages of sympathy and support from a far place. This reading, however, ignores his emphasis on seeing the utterance as something that is fully as social as the language system itself.

Two things should be particularly noted at this point. The first is that Bakhtin's idea of an utterance can normally be roughly equated to a speaking turn in a conversation. He points out, however, that these turns are of indefinite duration, ranging from a monosyllable at one extreme to the 'utterance' of a novel at the other. The other is that they are governed not only by what we normally think of as linguistic rules, but also by conventions of genre. Within literary studies, of course, they have long received a particular kind of attention, and rhetoric especially has been an object of analysis since antiquity. What remains to be done, Bakhtin argued, was to extend this attention to all genres, and to incorporate it in a truly comprehensive linguistics.

To do this, it is necessary to distinguish between primary genres, which evolve in normal workaday situations, and secondary genres, such as literary works, certainly, but also such other phenomena as scientific reports. What these secondary genres have in common one with another is that they incorporate primary genres but express them in mediated form. In a novel, for instance, there may be an altercation in a pub on one page, and a discussion of the weather in meteorological terms on the next. These genres are only experienced by the reader, however, as component and contributory parts of the genre that includes and gives rise to that particular novel.

Bakhtin explicitly states that it is in genres such as literary ones that we find the greatest degree of freedom of personal expression, whereas in such genres as military commands or business letters individual expression is restricted to the greatest extent. Implicit in his reasoning is the belief that the combinatorial possibilities of secondary genres give the greatest scope for this kind of individuality. Indeed, the logic of his reasoning (though he himself does not press the point this far) might almost be taken to suggest that the literary genre should be considered a tertiary one. My reasoning for suggesting this is that Bakhtin acknowledges that changes in primary, oral genres can affect secondary genres (such as the scientific); he also recognizes that genres such as the scientific can be embedded within the literary. Since the contrary is not the case, this must, at the least, put the literary genre in a uniquely privileged position as regards generic complexity.

I discussed earlier how Bakhtin emphasized the role of the listener in speech, pointing out that every listener is a once and future speaker, hearing responses to what he or she has just said, and constructing possible future responses even whilst the other's utterance is being delivered. Within certain genres, such as that of military command, the possibilities for response are highly constrained. In others, such as novel-writing, they are very much deferred; Tolstoy's 'turn' goes on a long time when we are reading *War and Peace*. They are also, self-evidently, restricted by the various forms of constraint that limit the production of novels. All this means that dialogue can be, and perhaps typically is, highly asymmetrical in respect of power relations. What I should now like to investigate, with the help of Bakhtin's categories, are the means that participants adopt to achieve a greater degree of symmetry, and the degree to which this is typically possible in the setting of an educational institution.

The first and most obvious question to be looked at is this: who actually selects the genre in the first place? The standard answer to this question is that the genre is normally implicit in the social definition of the situation – a consultation in a doctor's surgery, a massed shout of encouragement to a football team, or whatever. And in situations where the social definition is weak or lacking (I may not know whether the strange face in my doorway is a new milkman or a doorstep evangelist) Bakhtin tells us that our first step, as soon as we hear the first few words of the first utterance, is to try to determine what genre we are confronted with.

Yet, even if Bakhtin here is not underestimating the possibilities of the situation, there is the danger that we may do so. In the example I have given, it is of course open to me to make the first move and determine the genre. A friend of mine, spotting the religious tracts under a caller's arm, once made a pre-emptive move by inviting him to kneel down and join in giving thanks for a fine morning – a piece of generic overkill which had the intended effect of preventing a long exhortation. Even in instances (such as the majority of classrooms that I have any knowledge of) where the possibilities of initiating moves of this kind are more restricted by the deployment of authority, it is still perfectly normal to find that any number of other conversations in other genres are going on before, after, and frequently during, the officially sanctioned discourse. Where a total breakdown of classroom discipline occurs, some other genre may take over quite blatantly. In other cases, such as the one I looked at in Chapter 3, the take-over may be only partial, more the subject of negotiation, and a lot less overt.

The comments above relate to the situation in school classrooms generally. There is a feature of literature lessons, however, which, though not unique to them, takes the possibilities of relating one utterance to another to the furthest degree. If Bakhtin is right in suggesting that the literary genre is secondary, with all the flexibility and possibilities of self-awareness and reflexivity that his use of that term implies, then discussion of literary works must be capable of sharing at least some features of this genre. For example, comments on the work can be made with quotations from the work embedded within them. This is not just a purely formal question concerning the use of quotation marks; it concerns also the kinds of things that are being said, and the ways that are being found in which to say them. For Bakhtin, all normal everyday conversations possessed the characteristic of using the same words in different utterences with differing forms of expressiveness attached to them. In the discussion of literature, however, this is not just a feature of the discourse, but also its ostensible focus.

For Bakhtin a genre was a whole, an entity which had to be spotted as an act of primary recognition. There is, however, something of an issue when it comes to recognizing the move from one genre to another. This point can be made by means of comparison. We recognize the end of a sentence in print by seeing a full stop. We recognize the end of an utterance by hearing one person stop speaking, allowing another the possibility to start. How do we recognize the shift from one genre to another in the course of a school lesson? Clearly a simple measurement of time, such as everything that is said between the ringing of one bell and the next, will not do. Sometimes it may be easy; a classroom performance of a play may be interrupted by a fire drill, with the necessarily brisk commands that accompany it. On other occasions the boundaries may be more difficult to determine.

Questions of boundaries between genres cannot be divorced from questions relating to the way in which we recognize different genres in the first place. It is both the strength and the weakness of Bakhtin's concept of genre that it allows for the possibilities of change in their constitution. The set of possible genres is not restricted to a given number, and the set of actual genres is being continually changed by addition. Presumably, too, a number of genres are constantly falling out of use as well, though this is not to say by any means that the number available at any one time remains constant. How, though, do new ones come into existence? Equally importantly, how do people recognize them once they have come to exist? Some changes in language, such as those at the phonetic level, may happen relatively quickly, but do not occur literally overnight. This, however, can presumably be the case with the creation of a new genre, especially if it is produced by combinatorial means out of pre-existing ingredients of utterances. But, if this does happen one evening, other people have to be brought to recognize it the next morning. That is the most urgent problem; the more diffuse and longer-term problem is to bring people to recognize that the repertoire of genres has changed. In genre, as in other aspects of the stream of communication, it is impossible to cross the same stream twice.

Even if we were to assume, however, that speech genres were fixed and immutable, Bakhtin's concept of how communication works would still allow for the possibility that one given genre might be put to a variety of uses by a particular speaker. Even in 'high' and restricted genres, where the possibility of variation is most restricted, the speaker can still introduce an emotional colouring into the way in which an utterance is produced. In the more fluid repertoire of oral genres, much greater flexibility exists. The selection of the way in which a genre is put to use in a particular context is the outcome of what Bakhtin calls the 'speech will' of the person whose utterance it is. Confusingly but significantly, he uses 'speech will' interchangeably with 'speech plan' to indicate that the concept embraces both the subjective intentions of the speaker and some consideration of the objective resources of the language. The listener, as co-partner in the dialogue, is concerned from the beginning to deduce what the speaker's speech will/plan may be, and it is this deduction, as much as any phonetic or other cues, that enables the listener to estimate when a speaking turn has concluded and another can begin.

What all of this suggests is that an increase in the knowledge and command of different genres, an ability to select and sustain an appropriate one for particular purposes, and a capacity to respond appropriately to a wide variety of common or relevant genres, should, on the basis of equity, form an essential part of the education of all pupils in the use of their mother tongue. Whether this is the same as the references in the English Proposals to 'speaking freely and audibly' is therefore a point that is worthy of frequent and continuing discussion.

If genre, in Bakhtin's use of the term, is as flexible and as subject to change as I have suggested, then it would require a very procrustean approach indeed to equate it with Foucault's concept of discourse within a disciplinary society. Equally, it would be an act of pessimism particularly alien to Bakhtin's nature to suggest that a repertoire of genres provides nothing more than the means to mount an ineffectual and complicit resistance. In avoiding this pessimism, however, I do not want to fall into the trap of suggesting that Bakhtin offers a ready route towards Increasing Your Word Power in order to Make Friends and Influence People. Speech will is not, and cannot be, as voluntaristic as that.

A more appropriate comparison might be to suggest the similarities between Saussure's view of *langue* as a given and immutable system, and Foucault's depiction of a discursive formation. In such a case, *parole*, with all its anarchic variety that nevertheless depends on *langue* for its communicative possibilities, would be the equivalent of the resistance that is parasitic upon power, and thereby poses no real threat to it. With both Saussure and Foucault, mysterious changes replace one system with another, without our having sight of any human or other agency that brings this change about.

If parasitism lies at the heart of the systems referred to above, then parody is the driving force within Bakhtin's scheme of things. The readiest means to modify an utterance, or a genre, is to use it with a different expressive intonation which expresses doubt or derision, where before there was certainty. Bakhtin frequently suggests that this was an important part of the dynamic of Renaissance literature, in which oral, conversational genres came to replace formal, written ones in a number of significant ways. However, parody is an insufficient name for the process, since what began as parodic genres then became substantive ones in their own right.

What is then created is an area of relative freedom in which the speaking individual can do one of a variety of things, but cannot do everything. The ability to disparage, to mock, to subvert, is built into the speaking situation from the beginning; it requires only a slight modification of the voice to achieve it. Establishing a dissenting and fully articulated point of view is more difficult, but aiding pupils towards the point at which they are capable of producing one is probably the primary responsibility of the English teacher. Reviewing the genres that pupils can use, and working to increase the number of them, may be the best way of discharging this responsibility.

10 Concluding

This book has dealt in a number of polarities, and this is a convenient point at which to list some of them. The picture of the free development of the autonomous individual, so powerful within the professional culture of English teachers, has been opposed by the notion of a common or an ascribed culture, conferring either benefits or restrictions, but in either event shaping or forming the individual sensibility. In a different way, the free development of the autonomous individual can be pitted against a skills-based notion of education, produced by an amalgam of the needs of the economy, of the future need of present pupils to move into that economy, and the assumed benefits to the individual of mastering a given set of externally-defined skills. If this takes place at the micro-level of the individual pupil, a somewhat similar polarity exists at the macro-level of subject departments and of schools, in which the traditional freedom of these institutions to determine their syllabus (modified in practice by any number of situational constraints) is contrasted to the externally-prescribed patterns ordained by the National Curriculum.

A rather literal-minded form of libertarianism (as well as other motives) can therefore cause teachers to spring to the defence of the autonomous learner and the autonomous school. That this is not a sufficient response to the situation is the contention of people such as Whitty, who argue that the National Curriculum is not just an imposition on the part of the state, but is a kind of contract concerning minimum standards and minimum content which it is in the common interest to oblige the state to deliver through a common schooling system.

However, it is at the level of the hidden curriculum that the polarities become most critical, and also most contentious. In the depiction by Foucault of the role of discourse in the formation of individuals and institutions, and in the various traditions of language study that see language as determinant in respect of the thoughts and assumptions of the speakers, we have a collection of theoretical bases for concluding that the freedom of the individual as a speaking subject is either highly constrained or non-existent. As against such a position, it is possible to construct a 'libertarian' Bakhtin (based, I would want to argue, on a very limited and partial reading of his works) who, stressing the freedom of the utterance in contrast to the systemic rigidities of language, upholds the creative freedom of the individual to produce a unique, willed, set of articulations in any given situation.

To some degree I have tried to argue against both of these polar positions. What I have tried to suggest, as far as discourse is concerned, is that it is various rather than uniform, and that different discourses, even if they broadly equate to one political party (such as the neo-liberal and neo-conservative discourses discussed in Chapter 4) can be in considerable tension one with another. The fact that such tensions exist calls into question some of the more globally pessimistic images of the disciplinary society to be found in certain sections of Foucault's writings, since it now becomes possible to think in terms of tactical alliances or strategic interventions, as the effects of one discourse can be brought, to some extent, to a position in which they work against the effects of another. This would then be more than just a doomed and complicit resistance.

Before this can happen, however, it is necessary for English teachers to rid themselves of some of the more autonomist notions of personal growth. This discourse has itself had a complex history, since it has most often been sustained by the same people who, in only slightly different contexts, have argued that language is profoundly important in shaping the thoughts of their pupils. What seems in practice to happen at this point is that people subscribe to the Saussurean distinction between language (*langue*) and speech (*parole*), accepting the language system as an incontestable given, but believing that the individual utterance is subject to completely unpredictable variation beyond the scope of linguistic investigation.

As I have suggested, I would prefer to follow Bakhtin in placing a third element, genre, between the poles of language and speech. The importance of genre, as discussed in Chapter 9, is that it is both a constraint (there is only a given range of genres available to and deployable by a given speaker at a given time) and a possibility (the speaker can select, can shift from one genre to another, and can even, by parody or by vocal inflection, modify or subvert a genre chosen by another speaker).

In attaching this value to genre I am to all appearances saying something very similar to the English Proposals for Ages 5 to 16, which refer, in summarizing Attainment Targets 1 (Speaking and Listening) and 3 (Writing), to 'matching style to audience and purpose'. This apparent similarity is something that should certainly be dwelt upon for tactical purposes. Yet style, crucially, is not the same thing as genre, and it is important to be aware of the differences. Style, in Bakhtin's distinction, belongs to the domain of language, whereas genre relates to utterance, in which people have differing speech wills (a stronger concept here than 'purpose'). So, in learning a mastery of genre, pupils acquire something more than the tact, accommodation, and self-effacement suggested by that term 'matching'. They acquire the ability to plan and execute, to negotiate, to dissent, and to oppose. And these should be goals to which anyone who does not equate personal growth with a desirable quietism should be prepared to subscribe.

Genre can be both 'taught' and 'taught about'; that is to say, the skills of using a particular genre, or of selecting an appropriate genre, can be developed, and pupils can be brought to recognize at a conscious level that such things as genres exist, and that there are skills of selection and deployment that are practical and effective in social situations. 'Teaching genre' has always taken place, at a certain level at least; many pupils, over many years, have learnt how to write the business letter. What I am proposing, however, is attention to a variety of more enabling genres than this, and, in particular, a concentration on the oral genres that, as Bakhtin stressed, are more flexible and more amenable to creative adaptation. It is here that a genuine strategic alliance is possible between this type of curriculum development and the approval for oracy that the National Curriculum expresses.

But there is also a place for 'teaching about' genre in the English curriculum. Here, as in other areas, there can be for the pupils a significant and irreversible step from the state of having an unconscious knowledge of and command over an (inevitably finite) repertoire, to the position of knowing something about the ways in which a (theoretically infinite) array of genres can be developed and used. And skills of this kind, once developed, can be applied to reception as well as production, and, in particular, to the literature component of English lessons.

With literature, however, the skills of recognizing and identifying individual genres are only one part of a complex of necessary abilities. For many of them, however, the concept of the 'speech will' is still an appropriate starting point. I can best illustrate this by means of a specific example. In Dickens's *Oliver Twist* we recognize (provided, that is, that we are moderately skilled and well-informed readers) a bundle of authorial intentions, such as the wish to give a quasi-realistic and unalluring portrayal of life in the London rookeries. We also recognize that this 'speech will' can be defined in negative as well as positive terms, as we come to realize that the absence of all overt reference to prostitution, and all examples of swearing, constitute a definite pattern. What we are doing here is making a comparison, based on our knowledge of social history and our awareness of the typical proportion of obscenity in certain oral genres, with the utterance as given, and concluding that certain absences are significant, and part of the speech plan that Dickens had in mind when composing the novel. The fact that characters such as Bill Sykes consistently utter imprecations that are not oaths may even lead us to conclude that this is a sort of parody, at a secondary generic level, of what we construe the primary oral genre would have been like.

But we can take the issue further than this, and consider the placing of *Oliver Twist* within a school syllabus, and within the canon of nineteenth-century novels (and the fact that the evaluation in these two cases would be somewhat different), and the selections and exclusions that have contributed to the compiling of these two lists, and the fact that 'English' is itself the outcome of a process of selection and exclusion – and conclude that 'speech will' is an inadequate concept, because tied to individual volition, for all that is going on here. What then becomes our subject matter is the series of social practices that have led to this subject, these lists, that author, that utterance, being prescribed for this place and time. It seems to me that a study of these questions is fully as educational for pupils as are the kinds of questions that are usually considered 'intrinsic' to the work in question.

A proposal such as I have just made is of course open to the objection that it goes a long way beyond developing language skills, or increasing appreciation of set literary texts. So it does; and so does the requirement that pupils should be able to talk about grammatical differences between spoken Standard English and a non-standard variety (Level 6 of Attainment Target 1). In both cases, what is envisaged is a knowledge about how language works and produces its effects; my contention would be that my proposal is even more empowering than the other.

Again, however, there is some possibility of a tactical alliance between the approach I have been advocating, and the requirement (even if restricted to Level 8) that pupils talk about the contribution that tone of voice can make to a speaker's meaning, e.g. in ironic and sarcastic uses of language. As a depiction of the many ways that oral genres can be used, this is decidedly limited, but at least it is a start.

But it is not only in the main body of English Proposals 5–16 that there is material relevant to our purposes. The document contains an interesting appendix (Appendix 6) based on work done by a group of heads of English departments. This consists of a list of 29 'approaches' (teaching activities, tasks, exercises, etc.) that class teachers might adopt when dealing with a novel on a 'class reader' basis – and the document as a whole makes it clear that it endorses the range that this appendix offers. It is indeed a stimulating range, likely to be of some help both to experienced and to new teachers of the subject. However, it is fruitful to try to categorize the different 'approaches' that are suggested. Some deal with the reader's perception of narrative flow; some invite empathy with the characters depicted; a number involve analogous modes of expression or paraphrase using different media. Only three, however, invite anything other than sympathetic projection or formal analysis. These are entitled 'investigative journalism', 'springboarding', and 'cultural contexts'. The first two of these involve the use of material extraneous to the text for comparative purposes, though the second of these still has 'empathy' as one of its goals. It is only in the last one that 'cultural and social assumptions' are referred to as determinants, and in all three cases the term 'authorial bias' is used, with the implication that any deviations from the objective reporting of truth arise from a mote in the eye of that particular novelist.

Motes do of course require prompt attention, but so do the beams of a cultural and social process that systematically privileges some works at the expense of innumerable others. None of us can undertake to study all the literary works that exist in order to carry out some kind of dispassionate empirical comparison that could lead to a selection based on godlike rationality and detachment. What we can do, however, is to look, as steadily as we are able, at how the process of selection and approval is carried out in the world that we know, and ask in whose interests it is being carried out. If we are able to form any conclusions, the interests of education and of equity may require that we share this information.

Further reading on
Bakhtin and Foucault

'The Bakhtin snowball is about to turn into an avalanche', wrote Hirschkop in 1989, discussing the secondary literature in the English language that was then increasingly appearing. Altering the metaphor only slightly, one might say that approaches to the Bakhtin corpus that are distinctly off-piste one season are covered with ski-lifts by the next. The introductory section of Hirschkop's bibliographical essay is very helpful in identifying these approaches, not only calling attention to the major difference between American and European commentators (the former often showing a tendency to see Bakhtin as a religious idealist philosopher, the latter more consistently depicting him as an innovative Marxist materialist) but also dealing with approaches such as feminism which, working from their own premises, have found Bakhtin a useful author with whom to engage.

A standard list of Bakhtin's original publications is provided by Todorov (1981, trans. 1984), who also provides details of English translations available at that date. Taken in conjunction, these two books provide a reasonably comprehensive apparatus for anyone who wishes to embark on a serious and detailed study of Bakhtin, as well as providing stimulating, and contrasting, commentaries of their own. The Hirschkop and Shepherd volume has the further advantage of providing a list of the various ways in which Bakhtin's key terms have been variously translated in different publications.

For the general reader wishing to approach Bakhtin directly, the best course of action is undoubtedly to start with *Marxism and the Philosophy of Language*. I would then suggest 'The Problem of Speech Genres' and 'The Problem of the Text' in *Speech Genres and Other Late Essays*. These could then be followed by the four studies that make up *The Dialogic Imagination*. Readers with a particular interest in literature might then embark on *Problems of Dostoyevsky's Poetics* and *Rabelais and his World*. It is only at this point that I would suggest attempting *The Formal Method in Literary Scholarship*.

For readers whose primary interest is to place Bakhtin in the wider field of theories of literature and communication, I would recommend Raymond Williams's *Marxism and Literature*, which, in addition to a section explicitly devoted to Volosinov/Bakhtin, is imbued with much of his committed and questioning spirit throughout. A somewhat briefer discussion is to be found in Terry Eagleton's *Literary Theory*.

The standard biographical work is Katerina Clark and Michael Holquist's *Mikhail Bakhtin*. The volume entitled *Bakhtin: essays and dialogues on his work* edited by Morson offers a representative sample of current American studies of Bakhtin.

A convenient list of works by Foucault, as well as of works about him up to 1984, is provided by Merquior's *Foucault* in the Fontana Modern Masters series, which also provides an acerbic though not totally unadmiring commentary that just about accepts the implications of the title of the series.

It can be helpful to start on Foucault by means of a representative selection of his writings, and Penguin's *The Foucault Reader* (ed. Rabinow) is just such a book. The section entitled 'Disciplines and Sciences of the Individual' has seven excerpts from *Discipline and Punish*, including one on Panopticism, and the volume also includes the essay 'What is an Author?' An alternative approach is via the various interviews that Foucault gave (though he often proved an even more slippery customer in these than in the books he wrote), and, with this caveat, *Power/Knowledge* (ed. Gordon), which includes the discussion entitled 'The Eye of Power' on Panopticism, can be recommended. In its bibliography it also provides a comprehensive list of interviews, articles, etc. up to 1979. Cousins and Hussain (see below) extend this to 1983.

However, anyone who has read this far in the present book should have no difficulty in moving directly on to *Discipline and Punish*. It would probably be useful to complement this by at least one of the loosely comparable books, such as *Madness and Civilization* or *The Birth of the Clinic*. Thereafter the next move might be to read *The Archæology of Knowledge*, which treats of Foucault's changing approach to his subject matter at this time, and has pertinent things to say about discourse. Finally ('. . . si vieillesse pouvait') the time will come to read the three volumes of *The History of Sexuality*.

Michel Foucault: beyond structuralism and hermeneutics by Dreyfus and Rabinow is a systematic attempt to introduce their subject to an anglophone readership. Somewhat more critical accounts are to be found in Cousins and Hussain, and in the collection edited by Gane.

Foucault and Education (ed. Ball) is, so far as I know, the first systematic attempt to apply Foucault's writings to the schooling process, and does so in a way that is likely to stimulate much further debate.

All the books to which I have referred above appear in the tabulation below, in which the accent is on availability rather than on comprehensiveness. Works by Bakhtin and Foucault are listed in order of composition (though, given the tortuous publishing history of most of Bakhtin's works, this statement must be immediately and seriously qualified); the publication date in brackets which follows refers to currently accessible translations as listed, and not necessarily to the first publication of the work in English. On the same principle, I have listed British rather than American publishers wherever possible.

Bakhtin

Selected works by M. M. Bakhtin

1927 (as V. N. Volosinov) (trans. 1976). *Freudianism: a Marxist critique.* New York: Academic Press.

1928 (as P. N. Medvedev) (trans. 1978, 1985). *The Formal Method in Literary Scholarship.* Cambridge, Mass: Harvard University Press.

1929 (as V. N. Volosinov) (trans. 1973, 1986). *Marxism and the Philosophy of Language.* Cambridge, Mass.: Harvard University Press.

1929 (trans. 1973, 1984). *Problems of Dostoyevsky's Poetics.* Minneapolis: University of Minneapolis Press.

1940 (trans. 1968). *Rabelais and his World*. Cambridge, Mass.: MIT Press.
1975 (trans. 1981). *The Dialogic Imagination*. Austin: University of Texas Press.
1979 (trans. 1986). *Speech Genres and Other Late Essays*. Austin: University of Texas Press.

Some works about Bakhtin

Clark, K. and Holquist, M. (1984). *Mikhail Bakhtin*. Cambridge, Mass.: Harvard University Press.
Hirschkop, K. and Shepherd, D. (eds) (1989). *Bakhtin and Cultural Theory*. Manchester: Manchester University Press.
Holquist, M. (1990). *Dialogism: Bakhtin and his world*. London: Routledge.
Morson, G. S. (ed.) (1986). *Bakhtin: essays and dialogues on his work*. Chicago: University of Chicago Press.
Todorov, T. (1984). *Mikhail Bakhtin: the dialogical principle*. Manchester: Manchester University Press.

Foucault

Selected works by M. Foucault

1954 (trans. of rev. edn 1976). *Mental Illness and Psychology*. New York: Harper and Row.
1963 (trans. 1973). *The Birth of the Clinic: an archaeology of medical perception*. London: Tavistock.
1964 (trans. 1971). *Madness and Civilization: a history of insanity in the age of reason*. London: Tavistock.
1966 (trans. 1970). *The Order of Things: an archaeology of the human sciences*. London: Tavistock.
1969 (trans. 1972). *The Archaeology of Knowledge*. London: Tavistock.
1975 (trans. 1977). *Discipline and Punish: the birth of the prison*. Harmondsworth: Penguin.
1976 (trans. 1979). *The History of Sexuality: an introduction*. Harmondsworth: Penguin. (Vol. 1 of the trilogy).
1977 (ed. D. F. Bouchard). *Language, Counter-Memory, Practice: selected essays and interviews*. Ithaca: Cornell University Press. (Rep. Oxford: Blackwell)
1980 (ed. C. Gordon). *Power/Knowledge: selected interviews and other writings*. Brighton: Harvester.
1984 (trans. 1987). *The Use of Pleasure*. Harmondsworth: Penguin. (Vol. 2 of the trilogy).
1984 (trans. 1990). *The Care of the Self*. Harmondsworth: Penguin. (Vol. 3 of the trilogy).
1985 (ed. P. Rabinow). (In Penguin edition 1986) *The Foucault Reader*. Harmondsworth: Penguin.

Some works about Foucault

Ball, S. J. (ed.) (1990). *Foucault and Education: disciplines and knowledge*. London: Routledge.
Cousins, M. and Hussain, A. (1984). *Michel Foucault*. Basingstoke: Macmillan.

Dreyfus, H. L. and Rabinow, P. (1982). *Michel Foucault: beyond structuralism and hermeneutics*. Brighton: Harvester.

Gane, M. (ed.) (1986). *Towards a Critique of Foucault*. London: Routledge.

Merquior, J. G. (1985). *Foucault*. London: Fontana.

Poster, M. (1984). *Foucault, Marxism and History: mode of production versus mode of information*. Cambridge: Polity Press.

Sheridan, A. (1980). *Michel Foucault: the will to truth*. London: Tavistock.

Smart, B. (1983). *Foucault, Marxism and Critique*. London: Routledge.

References

Apple, M. W. (1979). *Ideology and Curriculum*. London: Routledge.

Bakhtin, M. M. (as Volosinov, V. N.) (1929, trans. 1973). *Marxism and the Philosophy of Language*. Cambridge, Mass.: Harvard University Press.

Bakhtin, M. M. (1986). 'The problem of the text in linguistics, philology, and the human sciences'. In *Speech Genres and Other Late Essays*. Austin: University of Texas Press.

Balibar, R. *et al.* (1974). *Les Français Fictifs*. Paris: Hachette.

Ball, S. (ed.) (1990). *Foucault and Education*. London: Routledge.

Barthes, R. (1966, trans. 1977). 'Introduction to the structural analysis of narratives'. In *Image-Music-Text*. Glasgow: Collins.

Blampain, D. (1979). *La Littérature de Jeunesse*. Brussels: Nathan/Labor.

Board of Education (1921). *The Teaching of English in England*. London: HMSO (The Newbolt Report).

Bourdieu, P. (1977). *Outline of a Theory of Practice*. Cambridge: Cambridge University Press.

Bowles, S. and Gintis, H. (1976). *Schooling in Capitalist America*. New York: Basic Books.

Bowles, S. and Gintis, H. (1988). 'The correspondence principle'. In M. Cole (ed.), *Bowles and Gintis Revisited*. Lewes: Falmer Press.

Crowley, T. (1989). 'Bakhtin and the history of the language'. In K. Hirschkop and D. Shepherd (eds), *Bakhtin and Cultural Theory*. Manchester: Manchester University Press.

Department of Education and Science (1975). *A Language for Life*. London: HMSO (The Bullock Report).

Department of Education and Science (1988a). *Report of the Committee of Enquiry into the Teaching of English Language*. London: HMSO (The Kingman Report).

Department of Education and Science (1988b). *English for Ages 5 to 11*. London: DES.

Department of Education and Science (1989). *English for Ages 5 to 16*. London: DES.

Dixon, J. (1975). *Growth through English*. Huddersfield: Oxford University Press for National Association of Teachers of English.

Doyle, B. (1989). *English and Englishness*. London: Routledge.

Dreyfus, H. L. and Rabinow, P. (1982). *Michel Foucault: Beyond Structuralism and Hermeneutics*. Brighton: Harvester.

Foucault, M. (1975, trans. 1977). *Discipline and Punish: The Birth of the Prison.* Harmondsworth: Penguin.

Foucault, M. (1979). 'What is an author?' In J. V. Harari (ed.), *Textual Strategies: Perspectives in Post-structuralist Criticism.* Ithaca: Cornell University Press.

Foucault, M. (1980a). *Power/Knowledge: Selected Interviews and Other Writings 1972–1977.* New York: Pantheon.

Foucault, M. (1980b). *The History of Sexuality. Volume I: An Introduction.* New York: Vintage/Random House.

Foucault, M. (1982). 'Afterword'. In H. L. Dreyfus and P. Rabinow, *Michel Foucault: Beyond Structuralism and Hermeneutics.* Brighton: Harvester.

Himmelfarb, G. (1952). *Victorian Minds.* London: Weidenfeld & Nicolson.

Hoskin, K. (1990). 'Foucault under examination: the crypto-educationalist unmasked'. In S. J. Ball (ed.), *Foucault and Education: Disciplines and Knowledge.* London: Routledge.

Jackson, P. W. (1968). *Life in Classrooms.* New York: Holt Rinehart & Winston.

Johnson, R. in Education Group II (1991). *Education Limited.* London: Unwin Hyman.

Kafka, F. (1919, trans. 1961). 'In the penal settlement'. In *Metamorphosis and Other Stories.* Harmondsworth: Penguin.

Lynch, K. (1989). *The Hidden Curriculum: Reproduction in Education, an Appraisal.* London: The Falmer Press.

Murphy, R. (1990). 'National assessment proposals: analysing the debate'. In M. Flude and M. Hammer (eds), *The Education Reform Act 1988: Its Origins and Implications.* London: The Falmer Press.

Pechey, G. (1989). 'On the borders of Bakhtin: dialogisation, decolonisation'. In K. Hirschkop and D. Shepherd (eds), *Bakhtin and Cultural Theory.* Manchester: Manchester University Press.

Shipman, M. (1980). 'The limits of positive discrimination'. In M. Marland (ed.), *Education for the Inner City.* London: Heinemann.

Sinclair, J. McH. and Coulthard, R. M. (1975). *Towards an Analysis of Discourse.* London: Oxford University Press.

Torbe, M. and Protherough, R. (eds) (1976). *Classroom Encounters.* London: Ward Lock.

Torrance, F. P. (1962). *Guiding Creative Talent.* New York: Prentice Hall.

Whitty, G. (1990). 'The New Right and the National Curriculum: state control or market forces?' In M. Flude and M. Hammer (eds), *The Education Reform Act 1988: Its Origins and Implications.* London: The Falmer Press.

Willis, P. (1977). *Learning to Labour.* Hampshire: Gower.

Index